D1387706

PIERRE DEUX'S
FRENCH COUNTRY

PIERRE DEUX'S
FRENCH COUNTRY

BY
PIERRE MOULIN,
PIERRE LEVEC,
AND
LINDA DANNENBERG

Photographs by Guy Bouchet
Design by Paul Hardy

THAMES AND HUDSON

To the memory of
 Mady del Medico
To Alice LeVec
To Steven Sarle

Published in Great Britain in 1987 by
Thames and Hudson Ltd, London.
Reprinted 1988

Originally published in the U.S.A. in
1984 by Clarkson N. Potter Inc.,
225 Park Avenue South, New York,
New York 10003
Reprinted in 1988, 1990
Printed and bound in Japan

ACKNOWLEDGMENTS

This book was a joy to do, from conception to completion. The exuberance and generous spirit that characterize Provence and its style permeated our collaboration and remained undiminished through long, tiring days and temperatures that occasionally rose, under the Midi summer sun, to 107 degrees.

We have many people to thank, both in France and in the United States, for their guidance, cooperation, enthusiasm, and time.

For their interest and suggestions during the planning stages of the book, we are grateful to Michèle Le Menestrel and her organization, Les Vieilles Maisons Françaises; to Sylvie Hourdin and Christine Peuch, editors at *La Maison de Marie Claire;* to Esther Carliner Viros; and to Françoise Ledoux-Wernert.

The extended Pierre Deux "family," scattered throughout this country as well as in Paris, deserve particular thanks for their time and efforts well beyond the boundaries of their jobs. We are grateful to Stephen Jiavis in Beverly Hills, Connie and Gus Pentek in San Francisco, Diane Carroll in Carmel, Paul Reddick in Houston, Kathy Turman in Dallas, and Michael Meyers in New Orleans for giving us entrée to homes on their turf and for squiring us about during our visits. Our thanks go out as well to Anka Lefebvre in New York for her enthusiastic participation throughout the project and to Serge Bisono in Paris for his ready assistance on all sorts of urgent requests across the Atlantic. The research assistance of David Frost and Barbara Zauft during the latter stages of the book was invaluable and is most appreciated. We would also like to acknowledge the loyalty and fine craftsmanship of John De Deus, a man who exemplifies the best qualities of a true artisan. We appreciate, too, the expert advice of our good friend Jean Dive of Paris, an interior decorator whose superb taste has earned him world renown.

We are particularly grateful to all of the people who opened their homes to us, without whom this book would not exist. Among those in France who graciously invited us in: the Marquis and Marquise de Barbentane; Jean-Louis Brunet and his most welcoming family at the Mas d'Aigret in Les Baux-de-Provence; René and Andrée Burrow; Monsieur and Madame Denis Colomb de Daunant; Hélène and Pierre Degrugillier of the Mas de Curebourg; Dick Dumas in Les Imberts; Jean Faucon of the Atelier Bernard; Madeleine Ferragut and Nicole Barra, the "Antiquaires du Paradou"; Paul Hanbury and Robert Schootemeyer; Madame Julian; Jean Lafont; Madame Y. de Longpré of the Mas St. Roch; Monsieur and Madame Pascal Navarro of the Maison de la Tour; Monsieur and Madame Pechrikian-Raffi; Marcel Perret; Monsieur and Madame Peyraud, of the Domaine de Tempier, with fond memories of their world-class red and rosé wines; Tonia and Claude Peyrot, who opened not only their home in Moustiers to us but their faïence production house, the Atelier de Ségriès, as well.

We would also like to express our deep appreciation to the entire Deméry family: Charles and Annie, Christiane, Jean-Pierre and Christine, Régine and Francis; they were most generous in sharing with us their great knowledge and love of Provence, in allowing us to photograph the Souleiado headquarters as well as their homes, and in making us feel truly welcome throughout the weeks we spent in Provence.

In the United States we were welcomed by Ross Bagdasarian, Jr., and Janice Karman, Geoffrey Beene, Helen Gurley Brown, Virginia Campbell, Robert Domergue, Sandy Duncan and Don Correia, Mercès Freeman, Robert Grabow, Joan Graves, Tammy Grimes, Suzanne Hicks, Cathy Kincaid, Leslie Kohnke, Wayne and Lydie Marshall, Charleen Matoza, Milton Melton and Stephen Scalia, John Newcomb, Mr. and Mrs. Will Ohmstede, Jane Osgood, Charles Sanders and Ed Harris, Mr. and Mrs. Larry Saper, Le Somers, Sam Watters, Susan Wood, and Tim and Nina Zagat.

Several books were extremely helpful to us in providing historical background and esoteric style information. These include *Le Mobilier Provençal* by Henri Algoud, published by Charles Massin et Cie. in 1927; *Le Mobilier des Vieilles Provinces de France* by J. Gauthier, published by Charles Massin et Cie. in 1933; *Maisons Rurales et Vie Paysanne en Provence* by Jean-Luc Massot, published by Editions Serg in 1975; *Styles de Provence,* text by Jean Chaumely, published and distributed privately by Ciments La Farge, and *Mobilier Provençal* by Lucile Oliver, published by Editions Charles Massin.

This book would perhaps never have been more than a gleam in our eyes without the encouragement, guidance, and plain hard work of our agents Deborah Geltman and Gayle Benderoff. They helped our ideas take wing, and we owe them a profound thank you.

For the striking layout and design of these pages we want to thank Paul Hardy, a brilliant graphic designer who from the beginning loved the concept of the book and worked countless hours creating a distinctive presentation for our words and pictures. We want to thank as well Gael Towey Dillon, the gifted art director of Clarkson N. Potter, Inc., who supervised the visual side of the project with a keen eye and extraordinary care.

Finally, we would like to acknowledge, with abiding admiration, the editorial expertise, support, and friendship of our editor, Nancy Novogrod, whose fine touch and gentle suggestions honed the book closer to perfection.

Pierre Moulin

Pierre LeVec

Linda Dannenberg

February 1984

CONTENTS

An *allée* of majestic plane trees leads to the Château de Roussan.

INTRODUCTION

Provence, *until the end of the 15th century, was made up of a group of states separate from France, and in many ways it still is. Although it no longer uses its own language—Provençal—or maintains its own government, this earthy, fertile, sunbaked region of southern France has a character and style so unique, traditions so deeply rooted, and a* joie de vivre *so contagious, that it stands alone, a principality in spirit if not in fact.*

To find yourself in Provence is to be overwhelmed by an immediate and intoxicating assault on the senses. The air is heady with the powerful, aromatic fragrances of rosemary, thyme, and lavender; the radiant sun, huge and white, is so strong it seems to pulsate; the winds, from the gentle breezes to the relentless mistral, cool the brow and cleanse the air; and the chirping of the cicadas rings long after the actual song is over. Provence is a land apart, timeless, dreamlike. There is a quality of light here—the suffused, pure light that bewitched Paul Cézanne and Vincent van Gogh—that exists nowhere else, and a harmony of land, architecture, and people that is unforgettable. There are few places more perfect. Here a graceful flow of all elements—human, geological, botanical, and architectural—creates vistas whose colors, forms, and lines beguile the eye and soothe the spirit.

The style of Provence in every domain—furniture, architecture, tiles, fabrics, foods, interior design, gardening—reflects the richness, diversity, and character of the luminous land that spawned it. The earthy yet elegant look of Provence—*le style provençal*—has charmed millions of visitors and influenced thousands of decorators around the world. What has come to be known as the French country look is, in fact, the style of Provence. It is for this reason that, in writing a book on French country style,

A small hotel near Saint-Rémy, the Château de Roussan, is a classic example of an 18th-century *bastide*, or mansion.

These pre-Roman artifacts, left and above, dating from the 7th to the 2nd century B.C., were discovered buried in the garden of the Mas D'Aigret in Les Baux-de-Provence, and testify to the ancient heritage of this area. The tiny terra-cotta bas-relief and the iridescent blown glass vase were photographed high in the hills of Les Baux.

we have chosen to focus on the province of Provence and to present a cohesive country style, rather than to traverse the length and breadth of France, ending up with a country pastiche, mere variations on a theme. We also chose Provence because its style epitomizes the warmth, the imagination, the craftsmanship, and the charm characteristic of the French country look.

The popular image of French country style, we discovered, is quainter, more rustic than are many of the homes that can actually be found in the French countryside. While there are indeed lovely examples of quaint, rustically furnished cottages, there are also many other moods and styles tucked into the hills and dotting the plains. Our aim is to show that French country style is above all not a cliché. It can be as elegant as the wine producer's estate near Saint-Rémy; it can be as simple as the pink-washed cottage in Le Paradou; it can be as homey as the

sprawling ranch deep in the Camargue; or it can be as majestic as the Renaissance *mas,* or farmhouse, in the Alpilles.

The style of the French countryside has evolved over hundreds of years, passing through myriad design influences and arriving at a look that is appealingly genuine and perfectly adapted to its time and place; it is not a conceit imposed by a sovereign or a particular school of design. Within the cottages, châteaux, and farmhouses of Provence there is little effort to make everything "match," or even to maintain a continuity of periods. The French mix what they like with what they need with what

Bulls roam on a field in the Camargue.

the family has handed down. The look is eclectic and yet cohesive. The best of French country style is comfortable, graceful, and gracious —a mixture of color, texture, substance, and light that welcomes and charms in a way that is refreshingly open.

French country style is one that is open to broad interpretation, which is why it can be adapted so admirably. Nevertheless, it is a style that does have some basic markings. French country is not delicate crystal and porcelain, but rather the chunky, bubbly, hand-blown glass of Biot and the hand-molded faïence of

A cluster of canal-tile roofs characterizes the many small towns and villages that are nestled in the Lubéron region to the north of Aix-en-Provence.

Moustiers. It is not pale, embossed silks and satins, but vibrantly patterned cottons. It is not fragile gilded and upholstered chairs, but rather the rush-seated banquettes from Uzès, embellished with a naïf floral bouquet and designed for family living. It is not the sleek, symmetrical slate roofs of a Paris town house, but rather the undulating, mottled canal tiles on a patchwork of roofs tipped at odd angles in Lourmarin. And it is not manicured lawns with reflecting pools, but the rugged hills rampant with wild rosemary and towering, windblown cypresses of Les Baux-de-Provence.

Decorative style in all the French provinces incorporated and adapted the prevailing trends in Paris—the distinctive looks of the various Louis', Directoire, Empire, Napoleon III, and so on—resulting in regional interpretations after a time lag of several years. But regional style is more a product of the land and its people than it is of the mode of the capital and the court. It is determined by life-style, climate, geography, and available materials—practical rather than fashionable considerations. Provence was subject to many influences in addition to the trends from Paris. Enhancing the landscape, particularly in southwestern Provence, was (and is) the very visible heritage from the Phoenicians and the Romans, master builders

From Pinkerton's Modern Atlas, published by Cadell & Davies, London, 1809.

Set into jagged, bauxite cliffs, the 13th-century town of Les Baux-de-Provence, once the most powerful fortified town in the region, is a dramatic monument to the past.

Provence pastorale: in the rolling hills of the Basses-Alpes, near Moustiers, a hazy late-afternoon sun burnishes fields of lavender

with a great sense of style who left their enduring mark on the land from their thriving civilizations before and just after the birth of Christ. Later, in the 17th and 18th centuries, there were the craftsmen from Italy, traveling north to look for work, as well as the East Indian merchant ships that sailed into and out of the port of Marseilles, unloading their exotic and colorful oriental cargoes on the Provençal shores. But the influences on Provence were gentle. They served, for the most part, to expand rather than to transform the vision of the Provençal artists and artisans.

Nothing is subtle or understated in Provence, and that holds true for its decorative style. It is exuberant, lyrical, easy, even at times extravagant. In personified terms, Provence is not the pale, slim, enigmatic intellectual, or the purse-lipped dandy, or the impeccably elegant *grande dame* with the complacent smile; Provence is the effusive, laughing, handsome raconteur whom you feel you've known forever after ten minutes. Never stylized, never contrived, and never pretentious, *le style provençal,* in all of its manifestations, is distinctive, comfortable, appealing, and exquisitely crafted. The massive 18th-century walnut armoires, carved by local craftsmen in Arles or Fourques to last a millennium; the sensuous sculpted

stone mantelpieces of Apt; the brilliant, hand-blocked fabrics of the Souleiado firm in Tarascon; the aromatic herb gardens of Fontvieille; the bouillabaisse of Marseilles; the isolated, cypress-shaded farmhouses overlooking the Rhône valley; the imaginative country kitchens of the Bouches-du-Rhône; the stone barbecues of Gordes; the rosé wines of Bandol—all contribute to the singular style of the Provençal countryside.

Provence, like Gaul, can be divided into three parts—the Provence of the Rhône to the

Behind the Château de Roussan, an abandoned bakehouse overgrown with ivy and grapevines overlooks an unused pool that is surrounded by ample 18th-century peasant figures carved in stone.

A storefront-cum-residence in the old quarter of Saint-Rémy is typically Provençal, with its beaded curtain to keep out flies, abundance of potted flowers at every window, and a triple *génoise,* the three-tiered roof support fashioned from canal tiles.

west, with its Roman heritage and strong artisanal tradition; coastal Provence, washed by the Mediterranean and gateway, from the ports of Marseilles, Toulon, and Nice to all points; and Alpine Provence, poorer, rural, isolated, and austere. In the chapters that follow, we have focused on the Provence of the Rhône, specifically the triangle formed by Arles, Avignon, and Aix-en-Provence, a rich and creative area with a long cultural history, and without question the capital of Provençal design. We did, however, venture north, south, east, and west of these boundaries, for special homes, craftsmen, and events.

In the chapter "French Country Adaptations," we cross the Atlantic to the United States and journey from New York to Beverly Hills to show you how French country style translates, far removed from the hills of Les Baux-de-Provence. Since a wide range of furniture and products from many provinces of France, such as Brittany, Normandy, and Alsace,

are available and popular in the United States, while Provençal pieces are not always easy to come by, we feature rooms that incorporate elements from a variety of provinces, not exclusively Provence. Using provincial colors, fabrics, furniture, and decorative objects, as well as the imagination and warmth that characterize the style at its source, you can create the French country look virtually anywhere. The mistral may not howl down your chimney, and the sun may not be a shimmering aura outside your window, but the exuberant spirit of the French countryside will be within, and the charm will be there, too.

An apricot grove near Les Baux-de-Provence is sternly guarded by a scarecrow dressed as a gendarme.

A window opening onto and reflecting the rooftops of Moustiers is part of a recent renovation of an 18th-century house built into the cliffs that surround the town.

BEURRES VOLAILLES

ŒUFS GIBIERS

DETAIL CHIAPELLO GROS

FRENCH COUNTRY
COLORS

"My house here is painted outside in fresh butter yellow with raw-green shutters, and it sits full in the sun on the square where there is a green garden, plane trees, pink laurels, acacias. Inside it's completely whitewashed and the floor is red brick. And the intense blue sky above."

—Vincent van Gogh, *Letters of Vincent van Gogh*

The warm, rich, intense colors of Provence are the colors of the earth, the flowers, the sky, and the sea. They are colors that have inspired many artists and artisans, and for good reason. Brilliantly illuminated by the sun, which beams through crystalline air swept clean by the mistral, the colors are pure, true, incomparable. As Vincent van Gogh wrote in another of his letters from Arles: "The color here is really very beautiful. When the green is fresh it is a rich green like we rarely see in the north, a soothing green. When it is burnished, covered with dust, it does not become ugly for it, but the countryside then takes on gilded tones in all the nuances: green gold, yellow gold, pink gold, or bronzed, or coppery, and from lemon gold to an ombre yellow,

In the middle of a wheat field in the Vaucluse, a shepherd's hut, above, today used as a midday shelter by farm workers, is a humble structure with distinctive detailing —a soft red wash of color, white borders, and a _trompe l'oeil_ window.

Richly textured red bauxite hills in Maussane, below, frame the Alpilles chain in the distance.

Vast fields of aromatic lavender cover the Provençal countryside, right and far right, sometimes commercially cultivated, sometimes wild.

One of Vincent van Gogh's favorite subjects, right, the sunflowers of Provence—called _tournesols_ in French because their faces always turn with the course of the sun—here face west in the late afternoon.

the yellow for example of a heap of threshed wheat. As for the blue, it goes from the deepest royal blue in the water to the blue of forget-me-nots, to cobalt, especially to a pale, transparent blue, to blue-green to blue-violet."

The characteristic ochres, russets, silver-greens, cerulean blues, deep roses, alizarin reds, sunflower yellows, and lavenders of the Provençal landscape are among the intrinsic components of the French country look, picked up and adapted in furniture, fabrics, tiles, and interior and exterior décor. The gentle flow of color from the outside in and from the inside out—between the colors of nature and the colors of man—is another example of the harmony that typifies this area.

Old agricultural thermometers in a worn, muted green, above, adorn the russet barn siding of an estate in Maillane.

A former clock store, above, designed in the 1920s in Saint-Rémy, sports olive-green shutters and trim and contrasting white-striped red letters.

The white bauxite hills around Les Baux-de-Provence, which range in shade from buff to whitish gray, are full of marine fossils, above, remnants of prehistoric turbulence. A small house on a narrow street in the old quarter of Saint-Rémy, above right, the site of a bakery built in 1487, is enlivened by soft, blue-gray doors and shutters and lemon-yellow trough, planters, and sidewalks.

Even the weeds of Provence add beauty and a soft golden hue to the landscape, left.

On the property of the Château de Barbentane, near Avignon, 18th-century barn stalls with cypress green doors were labeled to identify the animals within.

The colors of a small house in Le Paradou, built in 1750, above, are inspired by the mineral-rich shades of ochre and red bauxite found in the nearby hills.

Red and white laurels, above, ubiquitous in Lower Provence, add vibrant splashes of color to village paths and private gardens.

A renovated *mas* in Saint-Rémy, left, was recently painted a deep, rosy pink and French blue, which will weather, after several seasons of sun and wind, into the desired shades of dusty pink and wisteria.

17

Vieux Nice, the small, intriguing town up behind the modern city of Nice, offers a kaleidoscope of colors and views. Here, more so than almost anywhere else in Provence, residents use a free hand and a free spirit in adorning their homes and shops with color.

In the hill town of Ménèrbes, a 16th-century house contains a foyer hand-painted in the 19th century with murals by a local artist. Similar murals once graced many houses in the area, but most now lie under heavy coats of paint.

In this view of the foyer, directly across from the armoire on the facing page, the powerful midmorning sun appears to be forcing the heavy door open. The designs on the ceiling and lower wall are the artist's charming naïve attempt to create *trompe l'oeil* molding and wainscoting.

Trellised grapevines, left, are dappled—and protected from pests—by pale blue copper sulfate spray.

The jade-green water of the Verdon River, below, flows placidly through the spectacular Gorges du Verdon south of Moustiers.

Fields of variegated greens, above—apricot groves, olive groves, vineyards—are bordered by towering cypress trees, planted to protect the crops from the wind in Les Baux-de-Provence.

At the annual Foire des Tilleuls, above, above right, and above far right, held the first and second Wednesday of every July in the small town of Buis-les-Baronnies, sacks of yellow-green *tilleuls,* or linden tree blossoms, are brought in by the local farmers to be weighed and sold. The blossoms, said to have calming properties, are a popular ingredient for herbal teas and natural cosmetics.

The soft, silvery green of olive leaves, left, is a popular exterior accent color for doors and shutters and appears frequently as well in Provençal fabrics and painted furniture.

FRENCH COUNTRY
FABRICS

In the dim and musty attic of the 17th-century Souleiado mansion in western Provence lie the heart and history of today's vibrantly beautiful French Provençal cottons. Here, carefully stacked and documented, 40,000 carved and laminated fruitwood blocks from the 18th and early 19th centuries form a rare working library of prints—from dainty to dramatic fruits, florals, paisleys, and geometrics. The collection is second only to that in the Musée de l'Impres-

sion sur Etoffes in Alsace. Souleiado, France's major producer of Provençal cottons, prints most of their fabrics industrially now, with some hand-blocking done to order; but whether the fabrics are printed on great factory rolls or hand-blocked on long tables by the meter, virtually every print currently produced is based on the designs carved by artisans more than 200 years ago. Although there are several other Provençal producers of printed cottons, such as Oulivado, a fledgling company, and Val Drôme, a small old firm whose fabrics are often made up into aprons or herb bags sold at local markets in southern France, none can compete with Souleiado in terms of quality or production.

The enormous charm of the fabrics results from the harmonious combination of three elements. At base, there are the high-quality cottons—over 150 threads per square inch, with a very fine warp and slightly heavier woof. Then there are the graceful, block-based prints, a curious mélange of naïveté and sophistication. And finally there are the warm and varied colorations, from subtle to vivid, inspired by the Provençal countryside.

World headquarters for these sought-after cotton

In an airy workroom at the Souleiado headquarters in Tarascon, right, hand-blocked fabrics hang from drying racks suspended from the ceiling. The cut copper block in the left foreground is used first to print a fabric's black outline; the colors are then printed sequentially— red, blue, green, yellow —with the numbered blocks in the background. Above, textile workers pose in the same Tarascon workroom, circa 1905.

prints are in Tarascon, a small old city on the Rhône, south of Avignon, north of Arles. Sequestered behind a high stone wall with green iron gates, La Souleiado, as the company is called locally, is an intimate, family-style operation, run by the venerable Charles Deméry, his wife, Annie, and his three children, Christiane, Jean-Pierre, and Régine. Charles, now in his seventies, acquired the company in 1938 from his uncle, also Charles Deméry, who purchased it from a Monsieur Veran in 1912. The Veran family had run the company since 1865, the year they bought it from the Jourdan family. A Monsieur Jourdan had founded the company in the late 1700s.

The company that the current Charles Deméry acquired was virtually unchanged from the days when Monsieur Jourdan ran it. It was a tiny enterprise, with five printers who still used vegetable dyes and the original wooden blocks. They printed only *mouchoirs*—large scarves—which they produced in three varieties; the *enluminés,* brightly colored, for girls and young women; the *grisailles,* in muted, grayed colorations for women "of a certain age"; and the *deuils,* somber-toned squares for old women and widows. On a good day they could turn out perhaps 100 *mouchoirs.*

While the Souleiado mansion still retains vestiges of the 19th, and even the 18th, century—the main stone staircase worn by 300 years of footsteps, the color-spattered laboratory, the attic full of blocks, lacy with cobwebs—the roots of the Provençal fabrics they produce go even deeper in history, back

Intricately quilted *boutis,* or Provençal bedcovers, such as this mid-19th-century one with its floral border, below, were once a traditional part of a bride's trousseau.

Provençal *boutis,* right, made between 1820 and 1870, air in the morning sun; particularly distinctive is the vivid cerulean blue *boutis* on the left, typical of those produced during the Napoleon III period (1852–1870). The yellow-glazed earthenware pot was made near L'Isle-sur-la-Sorgue in the mid-19th century.

into the middle of the 17th century. The beginning of the Western fascination with brightly printed cottons, and indeed the beginning of the modern cotton industry, can be traced to the creation of the Compagnie des Indes Orientales in 1664. Among the exotic merchandise the ships brought into the port of Marseilles from the East were brilliantly colored cotton print fabrics from India. The French were dazzled by the intricate patterns and striking tones, the likes of which they had never seen; they were almost equally impressed by the fact that the fabrics were colorfast after washing—a modern miracle in the 17th century. The imported India print cottons were unique and extremely expensive, which meant that they immediately captured the imagination and the gold *louis* (the coin of the realm) of the aristocracy and the *haute bourgeoisie.* They called them *calicots* or *chints,* from the Hindu words for the cotton fabrics, or simply *indiennes.*

The *indiennes* became a *succès fou* in Paris and at Versailles, the court of Louis XIV. Women had skirts, gowns, pinafores, and blouses designed from the fabric; men wore vests, dressing gowns, and doublets of the stuff; and all over the kingdom there were walls, beds, sofas, and windows covered with *indiennes.* When Madame de Sévigné went to visit her daughter in Provence in 1672, she brought a trunkful of the popular cottons as a gift. The fad grew to such proportions that when Molière played the foolish hero in the first production of his play *Le Bourgeois Gentilhomme,* presented for Louis XIV on October 14, 1670, he decked out his character in a rainbow of *indiennes,* some worn upside down.

Not surprisingly, soon after the tremendous response to the first Indian cottons, French textile producers set up ateliers to try to produce their own *indiennes.* The new industry, which many believed to be the wave of the future, drew artisans and other textile workers away from the silk and wool factories of Lyons, to the great detriment of the

The cherry orchard near L'Isle-sur-la-Sorgue, left, makes a serene setting for a summer picnic. The cherry-patterned *boutis* with a coffee background, in detail at right, is typical of the romantic quilts made in Provence between 1840 and 1850. The 19th-century pitchers and yellow faïence plates were produced locally.

28

old firms. The situation became so serious that many established textile companies began to founder, and by 1681 many were forced to shut down. There were riots and demonstrations in Lyons and Paris, with the owners of the silk and wool factories heavily lobbying King Louis XIV to do something to save their industry.

On October 26, 1686, the king banned by royal decree the production and importation of all *indiennes*. Stocks were seized and confiscated. Traders had to find new ports for their Indian cargoes. But instead of putting an end to the *indienne* craze, which most likely would have died a natural death like most fads, the interdiction fueled a craving for the fabrics that was even greater than before. *Indiennes* were smuggled in and sold for exorbitant prices; *le tout Versailles* were insatiable. In one of the century's most blatant examples of law being for "others," the *grands seigneurs* and *grandes dames* of Louis' court—those who were "above" the law— started up their own ateliers to produce the fabric. The Duc de Bourbon set up a large-scale printing operation in his château in Chantilly, while the Marquise de Pompadour gave her protection to a small

Swatches of 18th- and 19th-century *indiennes*, left, are part of Souleiado's extensive archives.

In the color-spattered laboratory of Souleiado headquarters, right, which looks as though it has changed little in 150 years, windows are permanently splashed with a kaleidoscope of experimental dyes.

community of artisans in Paris.

The ban was finally lifted by Louis XV in 1754. But for several decades before that, the law had been laxly enforced and new textile firms had sprung up and were producing *indiennes* without interference. Competition grew increasingly fierce to perfect the production of the fabrics, which were still vastly inferior to those produced in India. In 1734 the Compagnie des Indes assigned one of its young officers, Antoine de Beaulieu, to commit a form of industrial espionage in Pondicherry, India. They charged him with learning the vegetable dye recipes and precise printing techniques of the artisans whose fabrics they had been importing. De Beaulieu spent several months observing the process and prepared a thorough report, complete with fabric samples of every step.

When de Beaulieu's report was brought back to France, the domestic cotton printers were finally able to replicate the colors and the quality of the original *indiennes.* The key to the technique, it turned out, was the mordants (from the French verb meaning to bite), metallic salts that combined with dyes to form an insoluble compound on natural fibers. Added to the vegetable dye, then thickened with gum arabic to adhere to the fabric, the mordants made possible prints that did not bleed or run.

By the second half of the 18th century, the French were capable of producing superb printed cottons, Indian-inspired but reflecting the colors and flora of the regions in which they were manufactured. For the next 100 years the *indiennes* remained secure in their popularity, although styles and tastes changed. Under Louis XVI and after the Revolution, the most popular fabrics were those printed on a bronzy base and covered with flowers, vines, and herbs—they were called, in fact, *les bonnes herbes.* During the more stylized Directoire period, the fabrics of preference were geometrics with a surprisingly contemporary look—squares, stripes, and ovals in shades of mauve, olive, and puce. In the early 1800s, the tiny designs called *milles raies, pois,* and *petits cercles* came into vogue. These were the styles that enchanted Napoleon, and he bought basketsful for Josephine and the ladies of his court.

By the middle of the 19th century, with the burgeoning of the Industrial Revolution, the hand-printed cotton industry went into decline. Many small producers who had worked *à la planche*—by block—sold out to or joined the great industrial fabric producers who printed by machine. Great collections of carved blocks were burned as detritus of another age. Only in areas removed from the industrial mainstream—notably in lower Provence and Alsace—did a few companies continue to hand-print

Handmade copper measuring utensils, above, hang over the stone sink in the Souleiado color kitchen.

Régine Deméry, above, one of Charles Deméry's three children, develops a new design in one of Souleiado's studios.

Up in the Souleiado *grenier,* or attic, above, 40,000 hand-carved blocks from the 18th and 19th centuries are stored.

New Provençal cottons, below, are designed at Souleiado using components from old blocks. All prototypes are done by hand on cellophane.

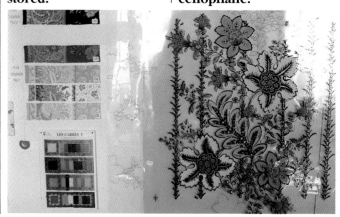

cottons for regional costumes. The classic *indiennes* remained out of favor for almost 100 years.

When Charles Deméry took over the company in 1938, he brought the operation into the 20th century. His first move was to change the name from the Charles Deméry Company to Souleiado, an old Provençal word meaning "the sun's rays shining through a cloud after the rain." The late thirties and the war years were quiet, marked only by a switch to synthetic dyes, since vegetable dyes were virtually impossible to procure. But after the war Sou-

Fabrics with burnt orange as a base or accent color highlight an eclectic veranda décor, combining Louis XIII, Italian modern, and wicker furniture.

In the elegant residence of Madeleine Ferragut and Nicole Barra in Le Paradou, modern Provençal cottons brighten exterior spaces. Oversized cushions covered in Souleiado prints, top, immediately draw the eye on a small patio. Rose, russet, and lavender print cottons, above, cover poolside lounge chairs, throw pillows, and the inside of the large, protective parasol.

In the kitchen of the Domaine de Tempier, above, an internationally known wine-producing estate near Bandol, hand-blocked Provençal border prints edge an above-the-sink shelf.

The fireplace, left, is also accented by the fabric, where it serves to keep smoke from fanning out into the kitchen.

leiado began to grow steadily, printing fabric by the meter for the first time and producing small fashion items such as handbags, skirts, and a few dresses.

As demand for their fabrics increased, the company could no longer continue to print fabrics by hand. From the fifties on, Souleiado began the slow transition to printing fabrics industrially, on engraved copper rolls. For the highest degree of authenticity possible, designs are transferred onto the copper plates complete with some imperfections —cracks or scrapes—from the original laminated wood blocks. Souleiado today offers hundreds of different design and color combinations, many in the vivid, traditional colors of Provence, others in newer, more sophisticated shades of moss, greige, dusty rose, apricot—what they call their fashion colors. All new designs created in one of the company's two small, airy design studios are based on original blocks. Final designs are usually compositions, taking, for example, the pinpoint background from one block, a floral accent stripe from another block, a paisley center from a third, and perhaps a scalloped garland from a fourth.

Souleiado prints only on natural fibers and is firmly committed to continuing the policy. "We will never print on synthetics," asserts Charles. "We have a two-hundred-year tradition of being cotonniers— cotton workers. We consider ourselves specialists and artisans. Most small printers sold out over a hundred years ago, and there are very few of us left. By printing only on natural fibers we are preserving our artisanal heritage. Besides, the prints are never as pretty on synthetics."

One reason for the remarkable success of today's Provençal cottons is that they are wonderful mixers. First and foremost, they combine beautifully among themselves, in a colorful pastiche of shades and patterns; in fact, traditionally at least two are meant to be used together—one fabric, usually in a simple, classic design, for the major portion of an item, accented by a floral border print from two to six inches wide. But the fabrics also go compatibly with a variety of diverse décors. They will complement a starkly modern living room done in neutrals, as well as a frilly boudoir in pastels. But, perhaps because of their oriental ancestry, they mix most splendidly with an oriental décor, remaining distinct but harmonious. However they are used, Provençal cottons convey a warmth and a welcome that is pure Midi.

A hand-blocked cotton square from India fills the foyer of the Domaine de Tempier; narrow floral border prints from Provence frame the doorway.

PROVENÇAL POTTERY

Because of an abundant supply of clay in the region, many small Provençal towns produce their own faïence—earthenware pottery with opaque colored glazes. The lines for the most part are fluid and classic, pieces ranging from simple demitasse cups to huge and graceful urns, used most often as garden planters. Traditional glazes are mustard yellow, emerald green, or opaque white with polychrome motifs. Faïence-producing ateliers flour-

One of today's Moustiers platters, produced using 18th-century techniques by the Atelier de Ségriès, depicts a maritime scene inspired by the designs of the great *faïencier* Joseph Olerys, whose production house prospered in the late 1700s; the rooftops of Moustiers on a summer day lie beyond.

ish from the mountains of northern Provence south to the sea, but a few, in towns such as Moustiers and Apt, stand head and shoulders above the rest, distinct in terms of quality and originality of design.

Moustiers, one of the greatest centers historically, is an ancient village clinging to the cliffs in the Basses-Alpes region of northern Provence. Since the 16th century, Moustiers has been a village of potters, but it was in the 17th century that faïence became an important local industry, particularly after a *faïencier* named Pierre Clérissy, a man descended from an ancient Provençal family whose members had been potting since the Middle Ages, established the first faïence production house there in 1679. Other ateliers sprung up soon afterward.

The pottery from the 16th and 17th centuries was classically blue and white, but in the 18th century a broad range of polychrome glazes was introduced. Still one of the most important faïence centers in France, Moustiers today has various ateliers that follow venerable technical and artistic traditions. All round pieces are hand-thrown and all flat pieces hand-molded out of red clay from Apt or

Among the collection of 18th-century Moustiers faïence at the Château de Barbentane, near Avignon, is this large cachepot filled with papier-mâché carnival masks from the early 1800s.

An unusual faïence candelabrum produced recently in Moustiers graces a country dinner table set with modern Moustiers faïence plates; the melons are the celebrated produce of Cavaillon.

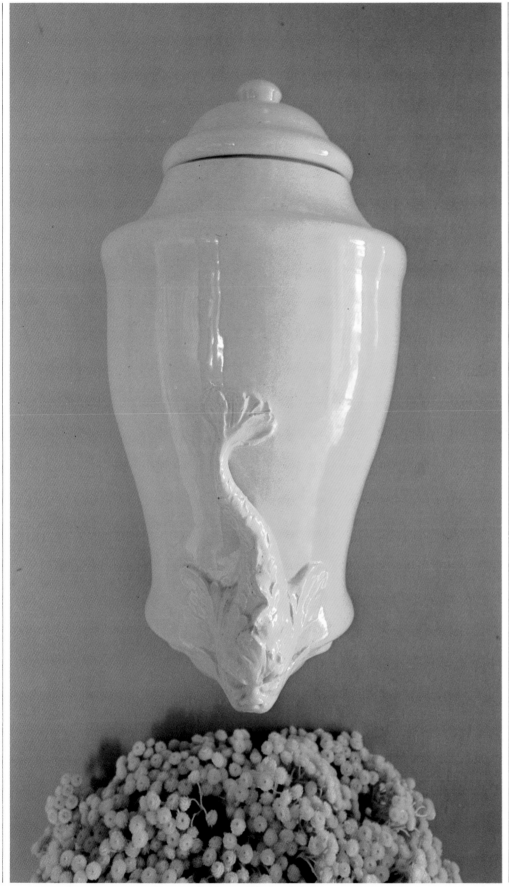

A striking yellow faïence watering pot from Aubagne is displayed to advantage against an olive green wall.

The creation of a
Moustiers pitcher: at the
Atelier de Ségriès a piece
of faïence passes
through many hands
and many stages on its
path to completion.
Working with logs of red
clay from Roussillon, an
expert potter begins to
moisten and mold the
clay into a cuplike form.

Working on a spinning potter's wheel and using a few rudimentary tools, the potter can throw a pot, or in this case a pitcher, within a few minutes.

41

Roussillon, then glazed in white and decorated by hand. The red clay under the white glaze gives the faïence of Moustiers its characteristic vibrant glow. Among the popular motifs adorning Moustiers faïence were—and still are—grotesques, or slightly deformed half-man, half-beast creatures, distant cousins to the gargoyles of Notre Dame, hunting or pastoral scenes, scenes from mythology, and, after 1789, revolutionary symbols and slogans.

Apt, once an important faïence center in the 18th and 19th centuries, now has only one major atelier to carry on the tradition. Jean Faucon's small, distinctive Atelier Bernard was established by his grandfather in the early 1900s. It was his grandfather who resurrected an all but lost 18th-century technique of creating faïence from colored, marbleized clays with a clear glaze. At first glance the pieces look as though they were simply covered by a marbleized glaze, but on close inspection it becomes apparent that the intricately swirling patterns are in the clay itself. The technique is time-consuming, and Jean, working alone or with one assistant in his tranquil atelier, can offer only a limited, highly sought-after production.

After loose flecks of clay are sponged away, far left, the pitcher is fired in a kiln, left, then cooled to await glazing, below.

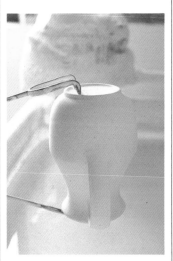

Using large metal tongs, the potter dips the pitcher into a vat of white glaze, above left. It is then sent on to the artist who outlines a classic design in charcoal using a perforated stencil, above, and then decorates each piece with colored glazes, left.

An artist, left, brushes on the colored glazes over the stenciled design. The job is a painstaking one, since one slip of the hand can mean the ruination of the almost finished faïence.

The pitcher undergoes a final firing in an intensely hot kiln.

After the pitcher cools from the last firing, it is either stored or packed for shipping to fulfill orders from around the world.

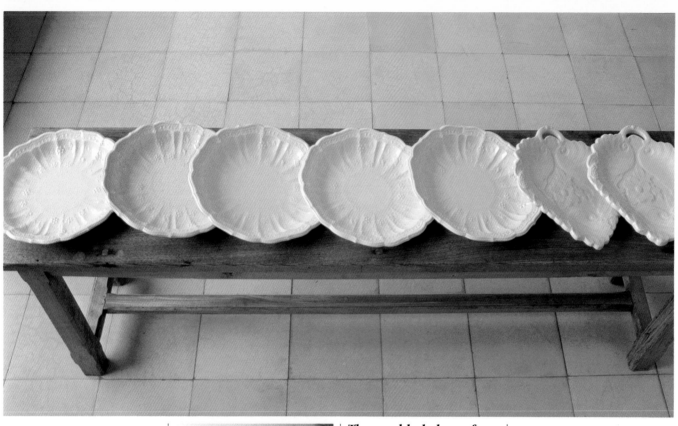

The yellow-glazed plates represented here, left, are among the characteristic ceramics of Apt. The scalloped round and naturalistic leaf shapes were hand-molded by Jean Faucon.

The marbled clays of Jean Faucon create faïence that is unique in the world; these pieces, like the blue-and-white plate and covered pitcher, sugar bowl, and dish, left, are finished only with a clear, colorless glaze; the intricate marbleized patterns are in the clay itself.

Jean Faucon's pitcher and basin, above, in marbleized brown clays are accented by grapevine motifs.

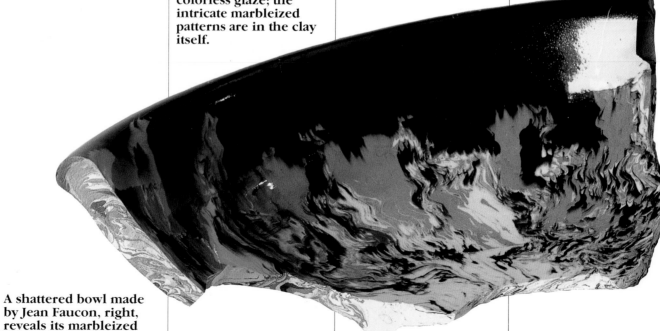

A shattered bowl made by Jean Faucon, right, reveals its marbleized heart.

A collection of Jean Faucon's marbleized Apt faïence is displayed on and above an 18th-century Provençal buffet.

A blue marbleized bowl with a scalloped edge is supported by a contrasting white pedestal.

45

Three rare 18th-century Apt serving pieces are part of Sylvia Etendart's collection in Sologne; the yellows, ochres, and browns of the marbleized clays are as deep and rich as any produced today.

The covers of six pots made in the early 1900s show the exquisite craftsmanship and artistry of Jean Faucon's grandfather, Bernard.

A simple scrub brush and Savon de Marseille—olive oil soap from Marseilles—form a still life near the sink in Jean Faucon's airy atelier.

After he mixes his clays (a secret process that no one is allowed to watch), Jean Faucon creates a small platter over a traditional mold, then allows it to dry in the sun.

Jean often works alone, creating only a few pieces a day.

After the clay is pressed over the platter mold, Jean adds the base, which at first resembles a skinny clay snake.

When the molding is accomplished, the marbled pattern reappears under the gentle strokes of a damp sponge.

The complete platter is set outside a sunny window to dry before being fired.

FURNITURE OF PROVENCE

No furniture combines form and function more gracefully than those pieces that are designed in *le style provençal.* Gentle, artfully curved lines, exquisitely carved floral detail, lacy ironwork, and deeply patinaed woods are the elements that make up Provençal buffets, armoires, chairs, and tables as well as the many smaller pieces with precisely defined functions, such as the flour box, the salt box, and the breadbox. The artisans of Provence used every opportunity to express themselves and display

their skill. Even the most utilitarian objects are ornamented with vines, wheat, ribbons, flowers, hearts, fish, or birds. As with Provençal style in general, the word "exuberance" characterizes the region's furniture. The cabinetmaker's love of movement shines through in pieces large and small, from a voluminous armoire to a tiny étagère, with expressive, undulating lines, sinuous curves, and softened angles. The play of light and shade is another significant aspect of Provençal furniture; in a land of brilliant sun, where light and shadow are sharply defined, artisans adapted the natural chiaroscuro to their furniture, juxtaposing straight lines with curved ones and deeply carved surfaces with mirror-smooth ones to catch and move the light.

Provence developed a refined and distinctive style earlier than the other provinces of France. Beginning in the 13th century, Provençal craftsmen created the pieces that were, and are, particular to Provence; the *panetière* (breadbox), the *farinière* (flour box), the

In a small house in Tarascon, a 19th-century *panetière* is paired with a very simple 18th-century buffet from Fourques.

Provençal furniture was produced by simple country carpenters as well as by great artisans. The rustic armoire of larch, below and on the previous page, painted in a soft gray-blue, was produced in Haute Provence in the late 18th century. It was designed to hold both clothes and grain.

buffet à glissants (buffet with a recessed upper tier), and the *garde-manger* (food storage cabinet). During this period, decoration was kept to a minimum, with perhaps a simple carved star or cloverleaf adorning door or drawer. In the 15th century, under the benevolent Provençal king René, local arts flourished, particularly furniture design; pieces that once had been simply constructed became expertly crafted and lavishly ornamented. By the 17th century, regional schools of style developed, particularly in Avignon and to the southeast in Toulon, where French naval officers supported an atelier of furniture designers. In the 18th century, Provençal furniture makers responded immediately to the sensuous, lyrical elegance of Louis XV style, identifying with its expressive, generous lines and unrestrained romanticism. It was then, during the reign of Louis XV, that Provençal furniture took on the lines and forms that today most characterize the style.

A close-up of the *pétrin*'s carved floral motif shows its graceful simplicity and the exquisite craftsmanship of the 18th-century Provençal artisans.

A *panetière* from the late 18th century—note the urn and fruit basket motifs—is set above a *pétrin* produced in the *fleuri* style of Arles in the mid-18th century.

The 1700s were an economically rich period for France; it was an epoch when provincial design all over the country flourished and, in Provence, a design trend toward opulent ornamentation bloomed. Toward the end of the 19th century, however, Provençal design became overwrought and exaggerated, losing some of its elegance, harmony, and balance. The turn of the century, with the advent of mass-produced furniture from the north, marked the decline of Provençal regional style and, indeed, the demise of French provincial design in general.

During the 18th-century glory years, much of the best Provençal furniture came from the area around the Rhône river, a department called the Bouches-du-Rhône. The land was rich, fertile, and profitable, and the locals prospered as well from the active river trade. Residents of Arles, Beaucaire, and Tarascon could afford to pay more for fine furniture. And since the Bouches-du-Rhône was where the money was, that was also where the craftsmen gathered. Two major styles, originating in

The centerpiece of the living room of the Mas de Curebourg in L'Isle-sur-la-Sorgue is a rare armoire from Fourques inset with a pendulum clock. Flanking the armoire are two 19th-century portraits of Arlesian women in traditional dress. On the left is a small walnut 19th-century night table. Also produced during the early 19th century, the humble walnut buffet, on the right, darkened by years of dust and smoke, is actually a very desirable piece today.

this area, particularly distinguish Provençal furniture —the style of Arles and the style of Fourques. The forms or silhouettes of both styles are basically the same, but the ornamentation is different. The furniture of Arles is the more elaborate, more highly worked, with ornately carved and curved lines and lavish floral detail. This style is sometimes called *fleuri,* or flowered. Sinuous carved moldings characterize both styles, but with the Arlesian pieces the emphasis is rather on the delicate, low-relief detail, such as garlands of roses, flower buds, and olive branches. Furniture from nearby Fourques, a smaller, simpler town, has less carved detail and ornamentation; craftsmen there favored deeply sculpted curves and undulating moldings with little or no decorative motifs. The effect is more vigorous, more architectural, slightly more rustic than the Arlesian look.

Other important design centers were Beaucaire, Tarascon, Avignon, Saint-Rémy, and particularly Aix-en-Provence, where craftsmen created luxe and

The detail of the armoire, above, created in Arles in the 18th century, displays a musical bent. Included in the carvings are sheet music, a lyre, two hornpipes, and a hunting horn.

This Louis XV–inspired 18th-century walnut chair, right, one of an extremely valuable pair, has been upholstered with part of a 19th-century tapestry. Note that each of the back supports is slightly different from the others, although at first glance they appear to match.

A small, early 19th-century wall cabinet in larch, above, from northeastern Provence, is embellished with drying herbs and flowers in a Moustiers kitchen.

A rare lacquer-green Provençal commode in the style of Louis XV, right, is part of the salon décor in the Château de Barbentane, southwest of Avignon. Pieces such as this were inspired by the lacquered furniture from the Far East brought into the port of Marseilles. Floral motifs in the style of Arles are applied in gold leaf. The framed portrait is of an 18th-century Marquis de Barbentane.

lavish pieces to satisfy a more sophisticated and somewhat more ostentatious clientele. To the north, in Haute Provence, which sheltered enclaves of Protestants in its austere, rocky environment, furniture design was more restrained, with straighter lines and few curves; pieces from this area are simpler, more rustic, sometimes more massive than those from Lower Provence. In the Comtat region and in the Cévennes, the contained, geometric style of Louis XIII remained a much stronger design influence than did the profusion of undulating lines promoted by his great-great-grandson, Louis XV.

Provençal furniture is adorned with an abundance of motifs, symbols, and design elements. On furniture created as part of a dowry, there are hearts (often on a palette with two hearts combined), kissing doves, myrtle leaves, and eglantine flowers (all symbols of conjugal love), sheaves of wheat (a symbol of prosperity), and vine leaves (a symbol of longevity). Other pieces are graced with almond branches, marguerites, bouquets of Provençal flowers, bunches of grapes, pinecones, farm tools, carafes, and fish. With the advent of Louis XVI, new symbols evolved—musical instruments, soup

A variation of the canopy bed, this *lit à l'imperiale* was in fashion among well-to-do Provencal families in the mid-19th century.

tureens, ears of corn, urns. Furniture from Haute Provence is marked by geometric lines and large *pointes de diamant* (diamond motifs).

Another important and characteristic adornment on Provençal furniture are the *ferrures*—the beautifully wrought and polished iron (or steel) work on armoire or buffet doors, cabinet drawers, étagères, and so on. The lacy, symmetrical *ferrures* are usually set end on end, in twos or threes, along the entire length of door or drawer. Extremely thin, strong yet delicate, the shining *ferrure* is another element that uses light to decorative advantage.

Perhaps most characteristic of Provençal furniture, however, is the wood from which it is crafted. The rich, glowing, honey-toned patina of the best Provençal pieces comes from the light, golden walnut that at one time was abundant in Provence but is now scarce. A firm wood that responds beautifully to the chisel and the awl, walnut is endowed with a color that is enhanced by age. (Plentiful though they

Ornate, almost baroque carving and lines, a style the French call *tourmenté* (tormented), distinguish this 18th-century walnut commode from Arles.

were in the 18th and 19th centuries, walnut trees were prized and were often given as part of a bride's dowry. Cutting down a venerable walnut in rural Provence was hardly a mundane event, and at times grew into a ceremony, sometimes accomplished under a full moon before a gathering of town folk.) Furniture makers also worked with other woods, but to a lesser degree: olive wood, used predominantly in the 16th and 17th centuries; pearwood, darkened to replicate ebony; willow for chairs; cherry, chestnut, and mulberry, sometimes mixed on the same piece of furniture.

There are several important, traditional pieces of Provençal furniture that no well-to-do home in Arles or Aix would have been without in the 18th or 19th century. Three are directly linked to the baking of bread.

The *panetière,* a uniquely Provençal piece created for the storage of freshly baked bread, is an elaborately sculpted cage with an elegant grillwork front and sides to allow the free flow of air. A small, deco-

This museum-quality example of a mid-18th-century *buffet à glissants* in the style of Fourques displays splendidly carved acanthus leaves, olive branches, and marguerites, as well as sculpted feet *à l'escargot.* Atop the recessed *gradin,* or upper tier, sit two 18th-century *pique-fleurs,* cluster bud vases produced in Marseilles.

This armoire with a *chapeau de gendarme* cornice is from the early 19th century. The three matching *ferrures* on each door balancing the three recessed panels are characteristic of classic Provençal armoires, particularly those produced in the Bouches-du-Rhône region, such as this one.

In a bedroom near L'Isle-sur-la-Sorgue, the painted bed, with sculpted laurel garlands and pomegranate motifs, was carved from beechwood in Aix-en-Provence around 1890; the bedspread is a 19th-century *boutis*. To the right sits a small, elegant Louis XV writing table of walnut.

ratively carved door opens out from the center of the grillwork. Although its tiny feet were initially intended to sit on top of a buffet or credenza, the *panetière* was soon suspended from kitchen walls, opening up more surface area and keeping bread out of the reach of foraging rodents. The top of the *panetière* is gracefully crowned by *chandelles* or *bobèches,* carved candlesticklike spindles symmetrically spaced all around. Provençal craftsmen loved to show off their virtuosity on this relatively small piece, and it often became the centerpiece of the kitchen.

The *pétrin* is a substantial, trough-shaped piece designed for the preparation of bread (*pétrir* means to knead) and was traditionally placed below the *panetière.* It consists of a trapezoidal chest with hinged top placed on a variety of bases, most frequently on four sculpted legs joined by an elegantly carved traverse, or occasionally, in simpler versions, on a plain, two-drawered table. Often part of a bride's dowry, the *pétrin* was used to knead bread and store it while it rose; occasionally the interior was used to salt pork. An extremely functional piece, the *pétrin* is less highly decorated than others, sometimes totally without motifs, sometimes with only a small carved design on its sides.

The *tamisadou* was also located in the kitchen. This unusual piece of furniture looks like a two-door cabinet but was actually created to refine and sift flour: it contained a *moulin à bluter,* or bolting mill, to prepare the coarsely ground flour for cooking, and had an exterior handle on its right side. The *tamisadou* is a piece unique to Provence and was usually simply decorated with scrollwork moldings and no floral relief carving. Today it is very rare to find one in its original condition; most have had their handles and mills removed and function simply as buffets.

In addition to the *panetière,* the *pétrin,* and the *tamisadou,* the Provençal kitchen traditionally contained several other classic, regional pieces. The *garde-manger* is a tall, narrow food-storage cabinet with a partial grillwork front resembling a *panetière.* This piece was often elaborately decorated with delicately carved floral reliefs, *ferrures,* and beautifully wrought hinges. Most have one door and a small drawer at the bottom. On the kitchen wall, usually placed on either side of the hearth, were two small decorative as well as practical boxes, one, the *salière,* for storing salt, and the other, the *farinière,* for storing flour. The *salière* has a slanted, hinged top for the salt and usually a little drawer on the bottom for pepper or other spices. The front panel is often carved with a crest or floral motif. The *fari-*

A classic 19th-century *litoche,* with a carved headboard and low posts at the foot, is covered with a 19th-century hand-blocked Provençal quilt.

nière is an ornate flour box commonly decorated on its sliding front panel with fish or wheat. It was commonly used to flour fish. To do so, it had to be removed from the wall and set flat on a table; the façade panel was slid off and the fish were floured within the box.

Also adorning the kitchen or dining area wall were various types of small étagères, specifically designed to hold dishes *(vaisselier)*, or glasses *(verrier)*, or pewter *(estagnié)*, or knives *(coutelière)*. All are self-contained units with bordered shelf fronts to keep displayed objects from sliding off. Sometimes they have backs, which were often covered with fabric to enhance the display, or else they are backless, creating a more delicate, lighter-looking piece, particularly for glasses. Some étagères have tiny feet so that they could be set on a buffet. A few rare versions look like miniature armoires, complete with small glass doors and *ferrures*.

The most spectacular and beautifully worked of all Provençal furniture is the armoire, a substantial and often intricately carved storage cabinet sometimes as tall as ten feet that was given as a wedding gift or included as part of a bride's dowry. On these voluminous pieces with fluid, curving silhouettes, Provençal artisans let their imaginations and skills soar. Classically, the armoire, fashioned out of light walnut, has two or three undulating panels per door in sculptural frames, richly carved borders, and ornate *ferrures* running the length of the doors. Supporting the armoire are either *corne de bélier* (ram's horn) or *pied de biche*

(doe's foot) feet. The cornices, particularly on those armoires created in Lower Provence, were often in the *chapeau de gendarme,* or policeman's hat, style, flat on either end and arched in the center. Armoires are rich in symbolic motifs carved in high relief or even openwork, among them turtledoves, hearts, torches, garlands of flowers, ears of corn, or bunches of grapes.

Lavish and elegant though they may be, it would be a misconception to think that all armoires were made for grand, or even comfortable, homes; many come from humble dwellings where they were the one valuable, cherished possession, handed down from generation to generation. Today the most prized armoires are those from Arles, Beaucaire, and Saint-Rémy. Armoires produced in the north of Provence, in the Comtat region and beyond, were somewhat simpler in presentation, with flat cornices, smaller *ferrures,* and less gracefully fluid lines; some have diamond-point motifs in the style of Louis XIII. Provençal housewives often lined armoire shelves and backs with *indienne* cottons, a bright and practical touch that gave the pieces interior as well as exterior interest.

A small 18th-century chair, right, hand-painted with flowers on an olive background, shows to advantage against the apricot wall of a bedroom in the Château de Fontarèches in Uzès.

This unique, majestically proportioned desk, left, was crafted near Arles in the mid-18th century. With its gently slanted top, which opens up for storage, it was probably designed for a lawyer or architect who needed a large work surface. Why the two doors, which do not exactly match, both open from the left is a mystery.

In a town house by the Rhône near Tarascon, a small, early 19th-century *encoignure,* or corner cabinet, below, is tucked under a recessed arched window.

A popular piece usually commissioned by aristocratic or *hautes bourgeoises* families, the *buffet à glissants,* a two-tiered storage cabinet, is another example of the Provençal cabinetmaker's artistry. Originating in Haute Provence but refined in Arles, this striking piece has a traditional buffet bottom, with two sculpted doors topped by a drawer—both adorned with elegant *ferrures*—and a recessed tier on top. The smaller, separate upper portion has two sliding *(glissant)* panels, usually ornately carved, and often a small curved door, or *tabernacle,* in between. The sliding panels were conceived as a way of storing or retrieving dishes or glassware without disturbing large tureens or vases placed on the buffet top.

Variations on the buffet theme include the *buffet à deux corps,* or chest-on-chest, which was usually proportioned for homes of majestic dimensions. The slightly recessed top part is often twice as high as the lower part on which it sits. These imposing pieces were popular in Haute Provence and are decorated with more restraint than the *buffet à glissants.* Some have two small drawers above the cabinet doors in the bottom portion, while the top portion is crowned by a *chapeau de gendarme* cornice. Another buffet, the *buffet crédence,* or cre-

A recently upholstered Provençal *canapé,* or sofa, circa 1845, reflects the sleek, fluid lines of the Louis Philippe style prevalent in Paris in the mid-19th century.

Four *farinières,* or flour boxes, above and above right, in different styles show a variety of ornamental motifs. Fish and wheat motifs are particularly characteristic of these traditional kitchen accessories.

denza, with two cabinet doors, sometimes arched, and small *ferrures,* often has a marble top. The doors usually contain recessed framed panels surrounded by molding. Occasionally in a Provençal home you may encounter a *buffet-mural* (wall buffet), which is actually a wall storage unit set into the wall with only a buffet façade. Some of these were quite small, tucked into a corner of the room, but others took up almost a whole wall—an early example of built-ins.

A typical and very practical piece of Provençal furniture, inspired by Louis XV, is the *encoignure,* a long, narrow, three-sided cabinet made up of one or two parts and specifically designed to be placed in a corner. Some *encoignures* have straight fronts, others have bowed fronts, but all have sides that taper to a point in back. Ornamentation on these pieces was generally limited to small *ferrures* and deeply carved molding and scrollwork.

Commodes, luxury items in the 18th century, were created for the living rooms or bedrooms of well-to-do families. They were produced in two distinct styles: with two drawers on long, curved legs or three drawers on short *pied de biche* feet. The façades were often bowed, swelling out in a series of convex and concave curves, and

This one-of-a-kind commode, left, in a rich, beautifully patinaed walnut, was designed for a particular space in a Provençal *bastide.* The three concave drawers have elaborate copper pulls fashioned into Provençal bouquets.

Falling somewhere between a *buffet-mural* and a spare room, this extremely rare built-in, right, called a *niche à toit,* is one of two (the other at the opposite end of the room is reflected in the mirror) located in the dining room of the 18th-century Château de Barbentane. Connected by a hidden passage behind the wall, the closets were conceived as storage areas, service quarters, and *cabinets de toilette.*

sometimes so ornately carved that the designs seem to writhe. The elegant hardware is fashioned from copper, bronze, or polished iron. Painted commodes, lacquered in deep greens or deep reds, were à la mode for a time in the late 18th century in aristocratic residences. These pieces, while they do exist, are very rare.

The Provençal bed, or *litoche,* is a simple affair, with an arching, gently scalloped headboard and generally spare, almost unadorned posts at the foot. In Arles, craftsmen designed a slightly more elaborate bed which had a sculpted headboard as well as a footboard, with the footboard sometimes higher than the headboard. Toward the middle of the 19th century a few very rich households commissioned canopy beds, or *lits à l'impériale,* with silk curtains suspended from a dome attached to the wall. In general, however, bedrooms were, and still are, quite simple in Provence and have never been a major interior design focus.

A classic, early 18th-century *radassié,* or banquette, sits opposite the wide fireplace in a 16th-century house in Ménèrbes; the room's original slatted and beamed ceiling is still intact.

All kinds of chairs for every spot in the house were produced in Provence, but most of them are rather rustic and simply designed when compared to the armoires and buffets they stood near. The most characteristic seat is the rush-seated banquette, or *radassié.* Traditionally placed near the fireplace, it sits three, and sometimes four, people and was designed for the convivial purpose of chatting. The banquette is constructed like three or four armchairs combined, with an arm on either end and seat backs that are gently concave slats. Occasionally the banquettes were painted an olive green, gray, or gray-blue and decorated with hand-painted flowers. *Indienne*-covered cushions sometimes rested on the straw seats.

Rush-seated armchairs are quite similar in design and construction to the banquettes. There are amply proportioned versions called *fauteuils à la bonne femme,* designed for grandmothers, and others with

The rustic 18th-century *vaisselier* is an étagère designed to dry and store glassware.

An unadorned early 19th-century buffet from Haute Provence serves as a showcase for an antique pewter collection in Gordes.

very high backs and low seats, called *chaises de nourrisse,* designed for wet nurses or nursing mothers. Seat bottoms are woven either of natural straw or of natural and tinted straw combined in an uncomplicated pattern. Under the influence of Louis XVI, the plain, slatted seat backs became more stylized, with framed motifs, such as a carved lyre or sheaf of wheat, joined to an upper and lower traverse. Furniture makers produced chairs from the traditional walnut, as well as from beech, linden, mulberry, or willow.

The majority of Provençal dining tables are simple, solid, and rustic and not particularly distinctive. For the most part they were purely functional, long and rectangular, sometimes with drawers on either end, designed for feeding twelve in comfort, if not in style. (Even in Paris no special dining tables were created until the era of Louis XVI.) It was the smaller, less utilitarian tables that inspired Provençal craftsmen—game tables, sewing tables, writing tables, dressing tables, night tables,

hall tables. Generally the legs of these pieces are long and emphatically curved with little or no carved detail, but their lines, inspired by Louis XV, are sleek and elegant. Console tables are somewhat more ornate, with marble tops, one or two drawers underneath, and a delicately carved traverse connecting the legs.

A fauteuil à la bonne femme, or grandmother's armchair, with a patterned straw seat and pretty carved detailing traversing the legs, sits in solitary splendor in the *réception,* or entrance hall, of the Château de Barbentane; it was produced in Arles and dates from the early 18th century.

Lavishly carved and cut out, the elegant commode, above, with the slightly bowed front is characteristic of the fine pieces that came out of Nîmes in the latter half of the 18th century.

A rustic 18th-century buffet, below, sports small, almost vestigial *ferrures* and simple carved detailing on the apron between the legs.

Mimicking the lines of an armoire, with its *chapeau de gendarme* cornice, the intricately carved étagère, above, with swags, flowers, and a dove was created in the late 18th century near Arles. The late 18th-century chairs, below, painted with ribbons and garlands of flowers on an olive green base, which flank a marble fireplace, have patterned seats woven from natural and tinted straw. The seat backs are *à la gerbe,* or in a wheat-sheaf design.

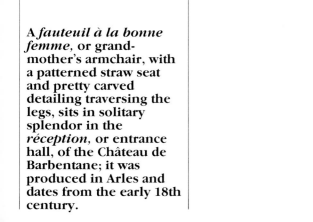

This fine, generously proportioned late 18th-century *banquette à trois places*—for three—adorned with flowers and a geometric gilt trim, is an example of the distinctive painted furniture produced in the Bouches-du-Rhône area and Uzès during the 1700s.

An earlier and more humble example of the genre, missing a rung and sporting a recently replaced arm, is the early 18th-century *banquette*.

Provençal dining tables are generally unadorned and rectangular, such as this one in the kitchen of the Château de Fontarèches in Uzès. Eighteenth-century rush-seated chairs painted green with gilt accents complement the more stylized décor of the rest of the room, yet are still harmonious with the simplicity of the table.

One half of a set of twin tables, a simple late 18th-century piece with a central X support is used to display some fine antique pewter.

ELEMENTS AND ACCENTS

The graceful lines and generous spirit of Provençal style mark not only the furniture of Provence, but the architectural elements, the decorative accents, and the crafts as well. There was no "design movement" in 18th- and 19th-century Provence, no guiding aesthetic theory, and yet all these random elements and accents have the harmony, grace, and coherence of a structured style. The artists, architects, and artisans who created what

grew into *le style provençal* did so in response to the needs, desires, and spirit of a people in a very particular time and place. Here we take a kaleidoscopic look at the essential elements and accents—including doors, windows, roofs, ceilings, floors, fireplaces, staircases, fountains, sculptures, *objets, santons*—that contribute to *le style provençal.* Used on their own or as part of a total French country look, all of these components are distinctive and immensely appealing.

In this land of powerful sun and staggering winds, **doors and windows** are designed to guard the interior from the exterior. Windows are almost always shuttered or protected by iron grills and are often quite small, such as the round *oeil-de-boeuf* (bull's eye) window, particularly on the northern side of the house. French doors, or what the French call *portes-fenêtres,* really elongated windows that open out onto a terrace or balcony, are also protected by long shutters. During the

A small brass knocker, doorknob, and latch add subtle visual interest to an ochre-washed door in the village of Le Plan de Castellets.

Beaded curtains, called *rideaux de buis,* allow air and some light in while keeping flies out.

day interiors are usually kept dark, with the shutters closed throughout the sunny hours and opened only in the evening to let in the fresh, cool air.

Both doors and windows, particularly those that arch, are often bordered by small, symmetrical stone blocks for eye-pleasing reinforcement. On door and window shutters alike, color is used liberally and with great zest; a heavy border of white paint sometimes frames the entire window casement. Doors can be massive, embellished with impressive ironwork trim, or plain, sporting only a dried sunflower.

Trellises covered by lush grapevines shelter many doorways, particularly in southern Provence, since shade during the searing summer months is at a premium. Another popular door accoutrement is the beaded curtain, called a *rideau de buis,* which allows air to flow through an open doorway while keeping flies out.

Matching wood-planked shutters and a door, above, accent a stone *mas,* or farmhouse, near Saint-Rémy.

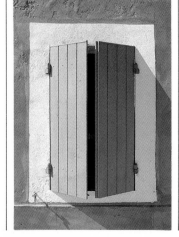

A fieldhand's entrance to a *mas,* above, is imaginatively constructed from two widths of vertical planks.

French blue window shutters of a restored Provençal *mas,* left, are half closed against the afternoon sun. The ramshackle door of a gardener's hut on an estate in Maillane, above, was long ago painted a rusty red to match the brick wall.

84

Large *portes-fenêtres,* or French doors, above, are protected by latching shutters. An 18th-century door with elaborate locks and ironwork, right, leads from a garden in Fontvieille.

An arched, heavily planked door and matching shutters vividly painted in turquoise add both protection and a striking visual accent to an 18th-century cottage in Le Paradou.

Seen through a garden archway near Eygalières, above, and close-up, right, an *oeil-de-boeuf* window framed in white tops a carved, paneled door bordered in asymmetrical stone blocks. The small window brings light into an interior hallway.

In a carriage house in Maillane, the shape, style, and molding of the double French door, left, is echoed on a smaller scale by the window above.

In the town of Les Imberts, a horizontally planked door, left, is studded with a variety of iron nails; the heavy oval door pull is of cast iron.

A classic French country look: lace curtains cover the bedroom windows of a small house in Tarascon, while hand-blocked Provençal cotton curtains remain open at the side.

A deeply recessed arched window is a late 19th-century architectural detail in Nice.

A simple muslin curtain covers a small bedroom window in Les Imberts, above. A plain shuttered window in Les Imberts, right, is topped by a triangular niche that was designed to allow in a small amount of daylight when the shutters are closed against the sun and heat of the Provençal summer.

In a restored 16th-century house near Gordes, a small hall window only inches from the floor, above, is protected by a single decorative wrought-iron guard. A tiny *oeil-de-boeuf* window, right, illuminates an artist's atelier built into the hills of Les Baux-de-Provence.

Late afternoon sun slants through large French doors opening onto a stone terrace in Maillane.

An arched village window is bordered by hand-carved blocks and protected by horizontally planked, iron-studded shutters.

The entrance to the *colombier* at the Château de Barbentane, near Avignon, top, bears a carved label. Below the *colombier,* above, cows and sheep were kept in stone stalls.

The large, turretlike *colombier,* built in the early 18th century, was one of the peripheral structures on the property of the château.

Another classic Provençal architectural feature, **pigeonniers,** also called *colombiers,* are seen all over the countryside, either as an extension of a farmhouse or as an independent structure. These sometimes enormous dovecotes were, and in a few cases still are, maintained as an abundant source of food; the pigeon droppings, which were in great supply, fertilized the fields. Some *pigeonniers* are simple structures, an unadorned pyramid of pigeonholes atop the barn, but others are surprisingly elaborate, architecturally unique and distinctive. The holes, which can be in the shape of hearts, clover leaves, or arches, are just large enough for pigeons but too small for other birds, such as eagles, that prey on them. The interiors are filled with individual pigeon roosts (in the largest *pigeonniers,* up to two or three thousand), like interconnected birdhouses, or a pigeon condominium! At one time the *pigeonnier* used to be closely linked with local law and custom—one was taxed according to one's personal pigeon population, for example—but over time the old rules and ways have been forgotten. No longer kept primarily for practical reasons or financial standing, pigeons today, in their unusual abodes, represent mainly a decorative hobby.

White pigeons peek out of the *pigeonnier* at La Belugue, a ranch in the Camargue.

The gently sloped and impressively durable **roofs** of Provence are typically constructed with terra-cotta canal tiles (also called Roman tiles, or round tiles). Produced from local clay, their tone can vary from tawny brown to brick red, which gives the roofs their mottled, mosaic look. The tiles are cast from molds today, as they were even in Roman times, but some Provençal locals like to relate that in a few small towns in the 18th and 19th centuries the tiles were shaped over the thighs of young women—which is why, the stories go, some tiles are very narrow and others quite broad.

Supporting most roofs is the classic *génoise*—from one to four recessed tiers of canal tiles—which is the most characteristic exterior element of the Provençal house. A liaison between the roof and the exterior wall, the *génoise* protects both from the penetrating mistral.

The *génoise*—recessed tiers of canal tiles supporting the roof—is the most characteristic exterior element of the Provençal house.

Overlapping terra-cotta canal tiles form the roof of a small modern house in Les Baux-de-Provence.

As in many country homes in other provinces of France and beyond, exposed-beam **ceilings** are typical in Provence. Massive, hand-hewn beams give a sturdy, rustic charm to cottages and *mas* from Montélimar to Marseilles. Today many residents leave the beams bare, but earlier in this century and throughout the last, it was the practice to cover all exposed wood with a heavy slathering of plaster. Often the walls, too, were coated. In a land with a tinder-dry summer where, nonetheless, central fireplaces were kept going all day for food preparation, the plaster coating served as a very important protection against fire.

Also characteristically Provençal is the slatted ceiling. The slats, called *rondins* in French, were placed close together and served as supports for the planks of the floor above. In more rustic homes the space between the slats was filled in with plaster, giving the ceiling an interesting striped effect. Occasionally the slats are used alone, but more often the ceiling is given additional support by heavy beams.

In a restored house in Les Bories, near Gordes, old hand-hewn beams add Provençal character to the light-bathed dining room.

The rustic *rondins,* or ceiling slats, of the Mas de Curebourg in L'Isle-sur-la-Sorgue also serve as supports for the floor above.

The owners of the restored house in Les Bories built a new ceiling above the existing beams in the second-floor living room.

These two rooms, a kitchen in Moustiers, above, and a living room in Le Paradou, right, are examples of recent restorations using vintage slats or beams. The rooms themselves are modern while most of the components are from the 18th and 19th centuries.

A skylight illuminates the heavily beamed top-floor kitchen of a narrow, four-story house in Moustiers that was built into the side of a cliff.

As the roof and its *génoise* are the most characteristic exterior element of the Provençal house, the tile floors and other decorative **tile work** are the most characteristic interior elements. Since clay was and is more abundant in Provence than wood, terra-cotta tiles, either natural or glazed, are an economical choice for flooring. They have other advantages as well: They remain cool in summer and retain heat in winter, and are easy to clean. The tiles come in all shapes and sizes—large and small squares, rectangles, and hexagons, the last of which first appeared in the 18th century. They also run the gamut from rustic to highly elaborate, laid in polychrome or geometric patterns. (Marble tile floors are more unusual, and are seen mostly in the residences of the wealthy or aristocratic constructed in the late 17th or 18th century, such as the Château de Barbentane.)

The bathroom of the Château de Fontarèches in Uzès has a slatted ceiling and a terra-cotta tile floor.

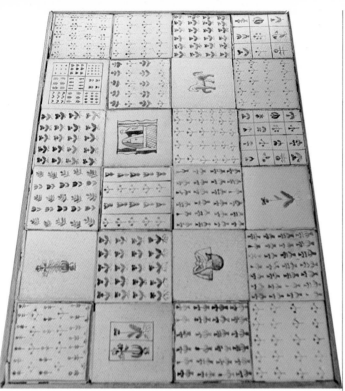

Hand-decorated white-and-blue ceramic tiles have been used to fashion the top of a terrace serving cart, above.

Large tiles glazed a lush deep green make up the kitchen counter, below, at the Château de Fontarèches in Uzès.

At the Château de Barbentane, the current marquis discovered a box of 18th-century glazed tiles in his attic and with them created a tile path to his pool, right.

In the chapel of the Château de Barbentane, 18th-century glazed tiles repeat a simple geometric pattern in groups of four.

Small, square 18th-century terra-cotta tiles run throughout a village house in Moustiers.

Even seen close-up, the *trompe l'oeil* marble floor tiling in the Château de Barbentane gives the illusion of depth and form.

Square terra-cotta tiles, burnished and smoothed by centuries of wear, cover the floor of a 16th-century town house in Ménèrbes.

Patterned floor tiles from the late 19th century adorn the foyer of a restored Renaissance *mas* near Mouriès.

Hexagonal terra-cotta tiles contrast with the lavender bathroom walls of the Château de Fontarèches. Portraits on the wall are Spanish caricatures from the late 19th century.

Two kinds of green enamel tile and two kinds of brickwork accent the fireplace of a rustic kitchen in the town of Le Paradou.

In addition to covering floors, ceramic tiles also adorn kitchen counters, walls, and tables. It is still possible to find old tiles in Provence from the 19th and even 18th centuries, some in very good condition, others understandably cracked. These tiles are widely sought after today to give character to a modern restoration.

Until the advent of gas and electricity, **fireplaces** were the heart of the rural Provençal home. They were the main source of heat as well as the cooking center, and, not surprisingly, symbolized security and well-being. In many homes there was only one common room where the family gathered to eat, work, and relax, and this room was built around the fireplace. (The French word *foyer,* derived from the word *feu,* or fire, originally meant a shelter that contained the fire.) Often the fireplace was the single decorative element in an otherwise extremely functional room, so it became the one area where an imaginative mason's skill could shine. Since each fireplace was designed for a particular space, no two are exactly alike. Usually positioned on an east or west wall, some fireplaces are made of plaster, with simple moldings and rounded forms; others, considered more "important," are of stone or marble. Many are enormous—literally cooking alcoves—easily the height of a man, several yards long and many feet deep. They were designed to allow one to four people to sit within, usually *grand-mère* and whomever else she needed to help her prepare the dinner.

The hearth was equipped with storage niches for condiments, hooks for utensils and hanging pots,

Marble floors in the contiguous salons of the Château de Barbentane were designed in *trompe l'oeil* style in the early 18th century and reflect the Italian influence prevalent at the time.

The medallion in the middle of the Château de Barbentane's central salon was created by Italian craftsmen using marble from Italian quarries.

The enormous fireplace, designed to allow one or two people to sit by the fire within, was constructed in 1768 at La Belugue, a ranch in the Camargue. The beehive-shaped openings to the right are the *potagers;* coals from the fire were placed inside, and above them, on metal grills, casseroles were set to cook slowly through the day.

large andirons, and a spit. So symbolic was the hearth in early Provençal life that a rural family was not considered to have taken possession of a new house until they had hung up the *crémaillère,* or iron pot hanger, in the fireplace. The act was as official as the signing of closing papers today.

U sually rather simple affairs, **staircases** in Provence are often fashioned out of stone or of terra-cotta tiles, since wood was in short supply and thus expensive. Some interior stairways are very narrow gauge, their dimensions adapted to a small corner or hallway. Handrails are carved in stone, worked in graceful wrought iron, or occasionally molded in plaster. Exterior staircases, designed to allow access to second-floor entryways, were frequently carved for the space by a local mason; many rise parallel to the exterior wall, very often attached to it.

The fireplace in a Moustiers restoration was inspired by a photograph of a similar one in the very thorough architectural reference book, *Maisons Rurales et Vie Paysanne en Provence,* by Jean-Luc Massot (Editions Serg, 1975).

A classic Louis XV fireplace was built into a 19th-century farmhouse near Eygalières.

Outside the house that was the first *mairie,* or town hall, in Fontvieille after the Revolution, above, an unusual rounded stone staircase leads to a second-floor entrance. An interior stone staircase, right, connects the first and second floors of a town house in Ménèrbes, built in the 16th century.

Extremely narrow and
designed *à l'escargot,*
this stairway, left, was
one of the original
components of a *mas* in
Gordes, built in the 15th
century. A narrow 18th-
century stone staircase
with a massive stone
railing, above, hugs a
wall at the Château de
Fontarèches.

Water trickles gently from the imposing 19th-century backyard fountain of an estate near Saint-Rémy.

At a *mas* in Mouriès, a fountain at the foot of the pool is composed of a stone grinding wheel and a carved *tête de grotesque* attached over the hole in the wheel's center.

Nostradamus, the 16th-century doctor and astrologist who was born in Saint-Rémy in 1503, is honored by this early 19th-century fountain in the old quarter of the town.

In an arid land, **fountains** used to be a necessary luxury—a ready, decorative source of drinking water for the thirsty. Throughout Provence, fountains are ubiquitous, dotting village squares as well as large residential properties, and ranging from a single, spouting orifice to elaborate, moss-covered "waterfalls." In addition to providing drinking water, some fountains also served as troughs for horses, or washbasins, or a combination of the two. Even today, in some tiny rural towns, it is not unusual to see a group of women doing their weekly laundry in the basin of the town fountain.

The abundant stone in Provence inspired local artisans to create more than doorframes, stairways, and fireplaces with the material. Their skill and imagination, augmented by techniques

Robust 18th-century peasant figures carved from local limestone sit beside a small pool on the grounds of the Château de Roussan in Saint-Rémy.

A 19th-century cherub, left, catches the eye along a private garden path in Fontvieille.

learned from itinerant Italian sculptors in the 17th and 18th centuries, manifested themselves in the many stone **sculptures,** used both indoors and out, that are so popular and so prized all over Provence. Carved from sandstone, limestone, or occasionally marble, the sculptures are romantic, allegorical, and sometimes religious figures; fruit or floral baskets were another favorite subject. Terra-cotta and wood sculptures, although much less common, can also be found in Provence.

No look at French country style, particularly in Provence, would be complete without focusing briefly on **animals,** both the literal and the figurative varieties. Animals have always been essential to the mainly agricultural Midi area—goats and sheep in Upper Provence, horses and bulls in the Camargue, swans and peacocks at the châteaux of Lower Provence, hens and roosters on the farms, dogs and doves everywhere. In their homes, the people of Provence love to surround themselves with representations of animals—portraits in bronze, wood, stone, clay, and every other conceivable medium. The presence of all this fauna lends an earthiness to the style of Provence that is incompatible with fussiness or pretension.

A portly 18th-century cherub, below, hugs his wraps near the entrance to the Château de Barbentane.

Outside the Château de Barbentane, a late 1700s carved basket heaped with the fruits of Provence, right, decorates a stone railing.

A charming 19th-century peasant figure, once brightly painted but today worn back to the natural wood, is part of the private collection of the Maison de la Tour, an antiques shop in Fontvieille.

In front of the *mairie* on the main square of the tiny town of Le Paradou, a sculpture, which sits above a moss-covered fountain, commemorates a local poet named Charles Rieu.

A sculpted stone *tête de grotesque,* a gargoyle head, spouts water into an *abreuvoir,* or trough, which today has become a small floating garden.

An urn of flowers is carved into the side of a 17th-century chapel in the fortified town of Les Baux-de-Provence.

Carved in the 18th century, a whimsical sculpture of *le mistral* blows perpetually from the first-floor landing of the Château de Barbentane.

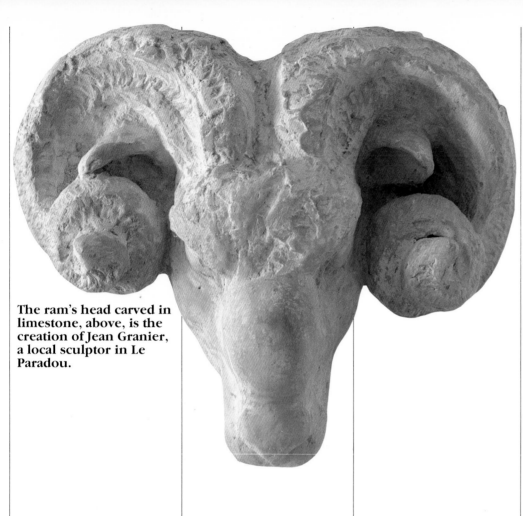

The ram's head carved in limestone, above, is the creation of Jean Granier, a local sculptor in Le Paradou.

A large swan and a flock of ducks, below, mingle in a stream on the grounds of the Château de Roussan near Saint-Rémy.

A small herd of goats, above, casually munch on the local greenery in Haute Provence.

Doves snack on grain in the barn of the Mas de Cacherel, below.

Bulls roam freely on the plains, above, bordering the mouth of the Rhône River in the Camargue.

A lizard, above, basks in the sun on a garden gate in Fontvieille.

At the Mas de Cacherel, a ranch in the Camargue, descendants of the wild white horses indigenous to the area, right, quench their thirst at sunset.

In the village of Avenos, a flock of sheep, left, is herded home at the end of the day.

A deeply patinaed pair of cast-iron cats, above, are terrace ornaments in Le Paradou.

Proud and aloof, a troupe of peacocks and peahens, below, have free run of the property at the Château de Fontarèches in Uzès.

A 19th-century bronze rooster, above, forged near Uzès, crows perpetually in a courtyard near Remoulins.

113

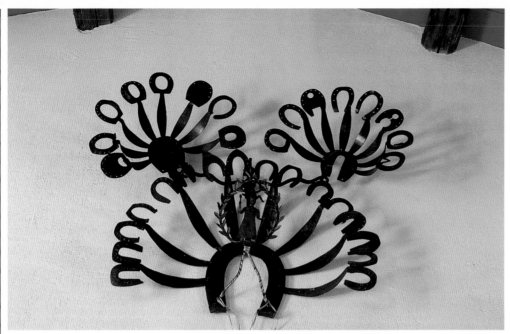

The interiors and exteriors of many Provençal homes, particularly the more elegant *mas* and *bastides* (country estates), are graced by **wrought- and cast-iron** detailing. Imposing wrought-iron gates outside and lacy wrought-iron handrails inside are especially characteristic of these grand local residences. The strength of the material and the delicacy and grace with which it was worked seem to appeal particularly to the Provençal esthetic. The *ferronniers,* or blacksmiths, of Aix-en-Provence, Avignon, Arles, Toulon, Uzès, Nîmes, and Carpentras brought ironwork to a high art in the region. The influence of Louis XV was felt in this domain as well as in furniture design. Before the Regency period in the early 18th century, wrought-iron gates and balconies were rather upright and severe in design; after Louis became regent and later king, the lines softened, growing fluid and graceful.

A delicate wrought-iron sculpture in a horseshoe motif, above, hangs near the ceiling in an Eygalières living room.

A wrought-iron lantern, illuminated electrically, above, bids welcome at the Mas de Cacherel in the Camargue. On the grounds of the Château de Roussan, the remains of a 19th-century greenhouse, its wrought-iron ribs almost bare of glass, right, are silhouetted against the sky.

A wrought-iron balustrade, above, in a classic swollen-front design reminiscent of Spanish ironwork, accents a small house on a square in Les Imberts.

A wrought-iron gate, below, offers graceful protection for a small home in Le Paradou.

A backyard iron lantern, below, lights a terrace dining area at a *mas* deep in the Camargue.

At a *mas* near Saint-Rémy, a wrought-iron lantern, above, hangs below a diamond-shaped aperture next to the entrance.

Near Mouriès, a rigidly designed wrought-iron gate, below, protects an elegant *mas*.

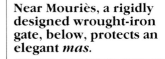

A former dressmaker's mannequin, below, fashioned of wrought iron, is propped against a wall in Les Imberts.

A hand-painted shield, right, set on a heavy wrought-iron gate marks the entrance to the Maison de la Tour antiques shop in Fontvieille.

The many small decorative as well as functional objects that come from this region can be grouped under the heading of **objets artisanaux.** They include such widely diverse items as birdcages, hemp filters for olive-oil presses, leather and straw boxes, straw baskets, hats, hand-painted mirrors, and rustic ladders. What all of these serendipitous objects have in common is a freshness of approach, a refined sense of color, and the characteristic Provençal harmony of line.

Charming, diminutive crèche figures displayed in Provence, not only during the Christmas season but often throughout the year as well, are called **santons,** or *santouns*, in Provençal, meaning little saints. The most traditional *santons* are quite simple, only a few inches high, fashioned out of clay hand-pressed into plaster molds and then hand-painted. Today, in addition to the still popular traditional version, there are extremely elaborate

The centerpiece of a tiny square in Les Imberts is a graceful cast-iron pump, left.

Scourtins, or hemp filters for olive-oil presses, below, are widely used in Provence as place mats, doormats, or wall decorations; set out on the mat is a new batch of *cerises au vinaigre*—pickled cherries—a Provençal condiment.

An elaborate 19th-century birdcage, above, now serves as a rabbit hutch in a yard near Saint-Rémy.

An early 18th-century leather box, above, with brass studs and angels, once had brass crowns and silhouettes of Louis XIV above the angels' hands and within the studs below the lock, but these were removed during the Revolution.

A 19th-century plaster ornament, above, adorns the walls of a salon at the Château de Barbentane; small squares of 18th-century *papier peint*, hand-painted wallpaper, cover the wall.

ones, some like big dolls, with realistic hands and heads of clay and beautifully detailed, handmade clothes. The *santons,* which have their roots in Italian nativity figures of the 16th century, first appeared after 1789 when the Revolution closed the churches and public displays of faith were banned. Jean-Louis Lagnel, an out-of-work sculptor in Marseilles, conceived the idea of creating tiny nativity figures for private family use. The figures were an instant success, filling a specific need for the frustrated faithful of Provence. There are all kinds of crèche figures, not only of the Holy Family, the Three Kings, and the animals of the manger, but also figures of everyone in the village—the butcher, the baker, the fisherman, the weaver, the old couple down the lane, gypsies, shepherds, millers, and musicians. *Santons* are a popular collector's item, and it is not unusual at Christmastime, when collections are fully assembled and dramatically displayed, to see a crèche in the corner of a living room made up of hundreds of *santons,* each one unique. One of the most popular places to acquire new *santons* is the annual fair called the Foire des Santons in Marseilles, where in late November, *santonniers* from all over Provence display and sell their work.

A collection of straw hats adorns the foyer of the Domaine de Tempier, left; in a Moustiers kitchen, right, two broad-brimmed straw hats accent a rough-hewn beam.

Delicate hand-painted pink and blue flowers and a dove embellish the charming 18th-century mirror, below, very likely a wedding gift or part of a dowry.

A rare and finely crafted *santon* from the late 1700s, above, has movable arms and a richly detailed costume of brocades.

A symbol of France, *le coq,* or rooster, is intricately stitched in this colorful 19th-century embroidered portrait, right.

All sorts of *boules à lavande*—lavender balls—to hold freshly picked lavender blossoms are available at local markets; those at the Buis-les-Baronnies market, right, are of ceramic or wood.

Design became somewhat overwrought in Provence toward the end of the 19th century, as attested to by the turquoise urn, above.

This rare early 18th-century Madonna, below, from southwestern Provence was fashioned out of papier-mâché; the soft colors of her flowing robes, patterned dress, and headpiece are original.

The skilled craftsman-ship of an 18th-century artisan is apparent in an intricately designed box, above, created from woven straw over wood.

A delightful naïve landscape, above, of the town of Beaumes-de-Venise, executed totally in glass beads, was created by a young woman in 1834.

This *santon*, above, created shortly after the Revolution, has extraordinarily expressive hands and an unusually detailed face.

Hand-painted sundials, such as this one in Maillane, left, are often seen on the sides of Provençal *bastides;* some simply indicate hours while others, much more complex, can show the day and month.

121

LIVING IN
PROVENCE

The finest Provençal homes, be they humble or grand, are true to their territory. In a shady village in the Rhône, in Vaucluse, Bouches-du-the rolling countryside of the or on the hot, dry plains of the Camargue, the houses are at one with the land—in proportion to their surroundings, constructed from local materials, and in character with their neighbors. Here, too, in the realm of

architecture and design, harmony reigns. In this chapter we visit six remarkable homes in Provence, each typical of the region, yet distinguished by its individual sense of style and unique spirit.

A MASTER'S HOUSE IN THE SPIRIT OF MISTRAL

O ur house is an *oeuvre d'amour*—a labor of love," says Estelle Garcin. "We collected furniture and *objets* for twenty years against the day when we found the perfect house. Finally, five years ago, it happened." Estelle and Emile Garcin discovered their dream house on the outskirts of Maillane, the rural town near Saint-Rémy where the Nobel Prize-winning Provençal poet Frédéric Mistral, who celebrated the land, life, and culture of Provence, was born and lived. The enormous amount of imagination and time the Garcins have put into their *maison de maître,* or master's house, is apparent throughout the property, from the sprucely landscaped grounds and immaculately maintained exterior to the personally designed furniture in several rooms and the magnificent home-dried floral displays almost everywhere.

In sight of the dining room windows, a massive stone table and wrought-iron chairs are occasionally used for casual, alfresco dinners.

The Garcin family's 18th-century *maison de maître,* or master's house, partially hidden by plane trees, was a stable very early in its existence. The off-white and soft brown colors of the exterior gently coexist with the house's green and greige surroundings.

A wrought-iron garden table and classic wicker chairs from Vallabrègues offer shady respite under a huge plane tree.

A graceful stairway, left and below, with an 18th-century wrought-iron banister, winds up to the second floor at the back of the black-and-white tiled foyer.

Within the house are all the essential Provençal ingredients in abundance—hand-carved stone, wrought iron, tiled floors, faïence, hand-blocked *indiennes,* regional furniture, basketry, and dried herbs and flowers. Air, light, and floral scents suffuse the rooms. Outside, sunlight and shade play over the intense greens of trees, ivy, and grass, the soft greige of the crushed local stone used as groundcover, the warm, weather-washed brown of the shutters and doors, the bright red blooms of potted geraniums. A paean to regional culture and taste, the Garcins' house in the land of Mistral exemplifies the spirit of Provence.

Above a grouping of potted plants by the entrance, a turn-of-the-century white painted wrought-iron medallion of Frédéric Mistral commemorates the fact that members of his family once resided in the house.

Just off the foyer, the creamy yellow dining room trimmed with white displays an impressive collection of turn-of-the-century plates. Covering the floor in the dining room, as well as in the other first-floor rooms, are large 19th-century granite tiles. The oval dining room table is encircled by a set of French turn-of-the-century dining room chairs in walnut. The ceiling, painted white, is a contemporary interpretation of the classic *rondins,* or slatted ceiling.

Collections fill the soft yellow-and-white living room as they do many other rooms in the Garcin house. Part of Emile Garcin's collection of naturalist paintings hangs on the far wall on either side of the fireplace. The contemporary sofa and chairs, upholstered in white wool, were designed by Monsieur Garcin.

Between the French windows of the living room, an English mahogany desk, left, holds a variety of writing paraphernalia and collected *objets,* including a circular bronze sculpture by Bruno Romeda.

In one corner a games table, left, covered with a vibrant 19th-century *boutis provençal,* is surrounded by English faux-bamboo chairs.

An international assortment of carved bears, right, is displayed in the living room on a table to the left of the fireplace.

Along one wall in the billiard room are shelves and glass cupboards, left, displaying an eclectic collection of *objets,* such as paint-brushes, apothecary jars, miniature sports cars, and 19th-century *santons.*

A round, portholelike window, left, casts a soft, diffuse light on a table covered with a *boutis* and holding, among other things, a collection of cigar boxes.

The billiard room, right, is chockablock with small collections and souvenirs of happy occasions.

The Garcins had a
professional stainless
steel stove and a tiled
work and storage area
installed within the
kitchen's original
fireplace, above. On the
mantel is displayed part
of Madame Garcin's
collection of kitchen
objects, right.

The stove is surrounded
by enameled ceramic
tiles and illuminated by
inset lighting.

The heart of the Garcin house is the large and fragrant kitchen, right, profusely hung with bunches of home-dried herbs and flowers. A Louis XV *buffet à deux corps* on the right wall takes the place of kitchen cabinets. Louis XVI chairs from Vallabrègues circle the table.

The drawers along the far wall, above, were once part of a local *épicerie,* or grocery shop. Estelle Garcin had false fronts about half an inch deep made for the drawers, which she filled with a variety of grains to show through the glass windows. Behind the fronts, the drawers hold kitchen equipment. For the slots where drawers were missing, Madame Garcin had straw baskets made to measure in Saint-Rémy.

A generously proportioned white porcelain tub in the master bathroom separates his-and-her sinks, bamboo wall cabinets, and bamboo-framed mirrors.

Near the bathroom window, a lacy rattan chair adds to the room's quaint but elegant oriental flavor.

A table by the window in an upstairs bedroom, covered by a *boutis provençal,* is set under two watercolor renderings of the Garcin home.

A TWO-HOUSE ENCLAVE WITH FAMILY TIES

In Le Paradou, a small village tucked midway between Arles and Saint-Rémy, Régine Deméry and her brother, Jean-Pierre, need travel only a few steps down a well-worn path to exchange visits. Their two small, colorful, and inviting houses are set several hundred yards off the main village road and are lushly protected from the winds and occasional passersby by cypresses, fruit trees, palms, flowering shrubs, and trellised vines.

Régine's rose-and-turquoise house is the older of the two, constructed in 1750 as both a barn and residence, where as many as ten people lived with their animals. Jean-Pierre's house, dusty pink and new-leaf green, was built around 1870 as a *bergerie,* or sheep barn; a new wing was added in 1950. The exteriors of both homes exhibit classic Provençal detailing—shuttered doors and windows bordered in white, canal tile roofs, and double *génoise* roof supports. The interiors reflect two very different individual styles heavily influenced by a shared Provençal heritage. Unpretentious, warm, and welcoming, both houses are, in short, *très sympathique,* just like Régine and Jean-Pierre.

The green of the horizontally planked shutters on both doors and windows, above, is in almost perfect harmony with the lush foliage that surrounds Jean-Pierre's house.

A small, well-worn path leads from Jean-Pierre's house to Régine's. In the distance, Jean-Pierre's wife, Christine, and son, Jean-Victor, above, return from a walk.

Régine Deméry wanted her home in Le Paradou, built in 1750, to be a very personal representation of her taste. Displayed on the kitchen wall is a collection of naïve oils and small plaster houses, below, which includes, at the upper right and lower center, her own house.

The vivid rose and turquoise colors of Régine Deméry's 230-year-old house, right, set back off a side road in the town of Le Paradou, reflect the bright, welcoming personality of its owner.

CHEZ RÉGINE

Régine Deméry loves vivid colors and she wanted her Le Paradou home, which she shares with her husband, Francis Azole, to be a very personal reflection of her taste. Covered in a deep rose wash with striking turquoise shutters, her house, which for perhaps the first two hundred years of its life remained unpainted, is exactly that. The interior, in stark contrast to the exterior, is painted entirely white, including the beamed ceiling, and in the living room large, square white tiles cover the floor. Lively, pink-splashed fabrics add vibrant touches of color to the living room, which is suffused with light throughout the day.

A long pine farm table, partially covered by a Souleiado cotton scarf and Portuguese serving bowls, stretches down the center of Régine's kitchen. The floor is unglazed terra-cotta tile; the fireplace is of recent vintage.

In Régine's living room, top right, a mélange of vibrant pink prints covering the chair, the sofa, and the oversized throw pillows enlivens the whitewashed walls and ceiling and white-tiled floor. The pink accent is carried through in the trim of the faïence cache-pots on the windowsill, in the pattern of the large vase above the bookcase, and in the detailing of the faïence end table next to the rattan sofa. In the bright and simple bedroom upstairs, center right, an old dressmaker's dummy wears part of a traditional Provençal costume. The armoire is English. Régine's newly refurbished bathroom, bottom right, is painted in ivory and accented with Souleiado tiles glazed with classic Provençal designs in green, off-white, and blue.

Jean-Pierre's Le Paradou home, built around 1870, was once a sheep barn; a large new wing was added in 1950. The soft pink color of the exterior walls, below, comes from the natural tones of the sand-base daub used instead of paint. At the far end of the house, a small bedroom, right, opens directly onto the garden.

A white, pink, and green paisley print by Sou-leiado curtains the small bedroom opening out into the garden, left. The handmade 18th-century Provençal bedspread is topped by Provençal print throw pillows. A table set on the small patio is ready to receive guests, right. Garnet-toned faïence plates are by M. Bichon, a cerami-cist in Uzès; assorted napkins and the table-cloth are stitched from Provencal cottons.

Old *santons*, a porcelain bust of an Arlesian woman, and glasses full of roses and mimosas form a pretty still life on the kitchen windowsill, right.

An unusual feature outside Jean-Pierre's house is a restored gypsy wagon, below, sometimes used for entertaining.

CHEZ JEAN-PIERRE

Juxtaposing Provençal elements and accents—tiles from Apt, Provençal cotton, an abundance of dried herbs and flowers—with English country furniture, Jean-Pierre Deméry and his wife, Christine, have created a distinctive and comfortable rustic environment for themselves and their little son, Jean-Victor. In contrast to Régine's house, the colors here are soft, with pink and apricot predominating; accents, however, such as the shutters outside and some tile work inside, are vivid. A highly unusual feature *chez* Jean-Pierre is the restored antique gypsy wagon in the front yard, sometimes used for entertaining.

A blend of Provençal elements and accents, English country pine antiques, pine-paneled wainscoting, and walls of soft apricot create a comfortable and eclectic living room. Sofas are loosely covered with Provençal print quilts and throw pillows. Hexagonal terra-cotta tiles are two hundred years old.

In the *réception,* or entrance hall, a dazzling patchwork created from multicolored enamel tiles from François Vernin in Apt makes a unique backsplash for a handmade ceramic sink, above and right.

The beamed master bathroom, partially tiled in glazed pink and white Souleiado-designed squares, has an unusual 19th-century *buffet-mural,* or wall cabinet, set into the wall; originally designed to hold china and kitchenware, it is used here as a linen closet.

PROVENÇAL TREASURE: A RENAISSANCE MAS

I n the middle of the 16th century, the wife of Les Baux-de-Provence's governor asked her husband to build her a weekend house not too far from the walled city. Instead of constructing one from scratch, the governor found an olive-oil mill five miles away in what is now the town of Mouriès, and had it converted into an elegant and roomy weekend retreat with Renaissance trappings. The work was completed in 1560.

Today, sheltered behind stone walls and iron gates, the Renaissance *mas* in Mouriès sits surrounded by acres of cultivated gardens and vineyards, seemingly immune to the passage of time. Among many fine houses in the area, this unique *mas* is a treasure, and has been classified as a *monument historique* by the French government. In each successive century additions have been made to the building, which has grown from front to back as well as laterally but not vertically. The distinct horizontal line of the house has been scrupulously preserved.

The present owners, a Provençal couple who bought the house in 1955, have accommodated their interior design on the first floor to the dramatic vaulted stone ceilings of the original oil mill. A neutral color scheme predominates while elegant French furniture from a variety of periods works in striking juxtaposition to the rough stone walls.

Although quintessentially Provençal with its mottled tile roofs, its plane trees, its sundial, its doorways surrounded by trellised vines, and its olive-oil mill heritage, this house stands alone. For in addition to its heavily Provençal characteristics, the *mas* is graced by Ionic columns, Renaissance friezes, and a line of elegant windows applied by a skilled architect in the mid-1500s and lovingly preserved in the rural Midi for more than four centuries. Photographs of this architectural gem have never before been published.

A unique Renaissance *mas,* snugly set behind stone walls in Mouriès, was converted in 1560 into a weekend retreat from a 14th-century olive-oil mill. Ionic columns were attached to the exterior walls of the second floor, as were friezes of Renaissance detailing below the roof, creating a Renaissance façade.

Adorning the western lawn of the *mas* is a long, scalloped garden, above. On the side of the house, a 14th-century archway into what was then the olive-oil mill is today merely an architectural remnant, left.

Carved Renaissance supports were attached at regular intervals below the second-story window ledge running the length of the original structure, left.

The serene and jewellike Pavillon de la Reine Jeanne below the walls of Les Baux-de-Provence, right, nine miles from Mouriès, was designed by the same architectural hand that in 1560 added the Renaissance façade to the Mouriès *mas*.

The mottled canal tile roofs of the *mas* slanting in all directions, above, are evidence of the structure's organic growth over several centuries. Next to the sulfur blue shutters of the caretaker's house, a crude sundial, right, indicates the hour.

In the dramatic vaulted living room, site of the original olive-oil mill, an eclectic mix of elegant French furniture from a variety of periods contrasts strikingly with the roughly textured stone walls and ceiling. Light from large table lamps bounces off the ceiling's curved surfaces and reflects up from the polished stone tile floor.

The color scheme in the living room has been kept primarily to shades of ivory and beige to harmonize with the natural colors of the stone floor, walls, and ceiling. A brocade loveseat, two modular chairs, and, along the back wall, an extended banquette provide casual seating. On the table in the foreground an antique glass bell jar encloses a butterfly collection.

Tucked into an olive-pressing niche is a mid-18th-century marble-topped commode from the north of France. In the foreground, Louis XV armchairs covered in a glazed cotton oriental print surround a contemporary smoked glass and steel cocktail table.

The centerpiece of the salon is an elaborate early 19th-century Clemente piano, left, its elegance in sharp contrast to the rough stone wall behind it.

A small nook off the living room, right, where ovens used to keep the interior warm in winter, has been made into a casual conversation area with a *boutis*-covered sofa, two Louis XV armchairs, a coffee table, and a hassock.

A stone niche beyond the living room, right, is set up as a small bar with two wooden shelves and an 18th-century *buffet provençal* as the base.

In the bedroom, above, lively floral print curtains and chair cushions complement the warm rosy tones of the terra-cotta tile floor, the 19th-century cherrywood armoire, and the 19th-century walnut writing table.

A monochromatic color scheme prevails in a corner of a small salon, above, with a beige lampshade, beige upholstery on the Louis XV armchair, and nubby ivory cotton and linen curtains.

Two resident terriers take refuge in the cool tiled foyer of the *mas,* left. The large 18th-century walnut armoire from Arles, on the left and in detail above, displays finely carved agricultural motifs.

By a bedroom window, an 18th-century *fauteuil à la bonne femme,* or Provençal armchair, flanks a round table draped in a 19th-century *boutis* and displaying crystal *objets* and a silver brush and mirror set.

IN THE VAUCLUSE, AN ECLECTIC VILLAGE RETREAT

The discreet façade of this tranquil village home, set on a tiny square in the Vaucluse region near Gordes, reveals almost nothing of what lies behind it—a long, L-shaped residence strung together from three small structures, a large interior garden with a rare Chinese mulberry tree, and a dramatic, sapphire-blue swimming pool. Built as monastery barns in the 14th century to shelter cows, chickens, and silkworms, the three structures became family dwellings after the French Revolution and eventually were converted into a single residence. Several years ago, American interior designer Dick Dumas, who has lived and worked in France for the last three decades, restored and decorated the house, carefully maintaining its Provençal character and sense of history while bringing it into a totally contemporary state of soft-spoken luxury and obvious comfort.

Under the sheltering mulberry tree a wrought-iron table with matching chairs is set for late afternoon cocktails à la Provençal. Set into the back garden wall are niches once used for keeping bees.

The lintel and border stones of this tall 18th-century doorway, formerly part of a local rectory, were purchased from an antiquarian stone dealer to replace the house's original low, unprepossessing entrance. The double doors open directly into a small library, with a view straight through to the garden.

In the living room, with the original heavily textured stone walls on two sides, a slatted and beamed ceiling, and white tile floors, there is a dramatic contrast between vital regional style and sophisticated interior design. A collection of oriental and modern art surrounds the 18th-century fireplace installed by Mr. Dumas.

A marble-topped 18th-century Provençal table backs one of three large identical sofas slip-covered in quilted muslin; the needlepoint pillow on the sofa echoes the pattern of the slatted ceiling.

The triangular wooden detailing below the ceiling of the small library, left, repeats the design of the triangular apertures in the stone beehives that are part of the rear garden wall. In the center of the library, a large sulfur ball, above, which once helped a 19th-century shopkeeper keep an eye on customers, reflects more than 180 degrees of the room.

The library, with built-in putty green bookshelves and a freestanding stone stairway, is the central room in the house, set between a small sitting room and the kitchen.

163

Stretching out behind the house, the dramatic swimming pool with its sapphire blue bottom is irresistibly inviting on a smoldering hot Provençal day. A silvery band of santolina runs the length of the pool on the south side, left. The white horse's head set at the far end of the pool, above, is a modern plastic-and-sand reproduction of a Roman statue.

165

In the master bedroom, the stylized canopy bed, designed by Dick Dumas, is fashioned from plumbing pipes painted in panther spots, above. Set between the glass doors to the garden is a small, graceful Louis XV writing table. Rusty-red-and-white print fabrics by Manuel Canovas drape and cover the bed; a quilted hand-blocked coverlet from India is folded at the foot, right.

Opposite the garden doors, a Louis XV Provençal armchair is covered in an Ivory Coast batik, right; next to it, displaying a variety of collectibles, is a wooden counter salvaged from a drygoods store. Clothes and linens are stowed in the built-in storage area with folding louvered doors.

In the one upstairs room —a bedroom above the library—inexpensive and durable dressmaker's muslin is used for the bedspread and pillow covers, below. The painted 19th-century French brass and iron bed belonged to the house's previous owner. An understated beige-and-white striped cotton fabric covers the Louis XVI-style armchair.

Within the house is an eclectic but balanced composition of 18th- and 19th-century French antiques, oriental art, and *trouvailles,* or discoveries, from local secondhand shops and flea markets. The house, with its personal and idiosyncratic collection of furniture and objects, was restored and designed as a retreat. To reinforce the feeling of privacy and serene seclusion, Dumas sealed up all the apertures facing out on the square, except for the entrance; the house looks out only upon itself and its thickly walled interior garden.

Small framed watercolors and engravings hang in the toilet alcove.

A collection of unusual turn-of-the-century mirrors in yellow copper frames lines the walls of the sleek cream-colored bathroom.

In the center of the bathroom the 19th-century bathtub, purchased in a junk shop, is encased in a local stone resembling travertine.

Muslin curtains billow in an afternoon breeze from the upstairs bedroom window, left.

Four lawn chairs designed by Dick Dumas are placed in a row by the pool, left.

A row of blue cypresses borders and protects the pool, left, from the wind on the north side. On the veranda are a sensuous metal-slatted outdoor sofa, right, and matching chair (not shown), both recent designs of Mr. Dumas.

Topping a garden wall at the south end of the property, a lineup of cherry conserves, below, cooks in the sun.

FRENCH MACHISMO: A RUGGED RANCH IN THE CAMARGUE

In a province of powerful color and light, the Camargue, at the southwestern tip of Provence, still startles with its colorful and luminous intensity. The Camargue is a special place, a land of cowboys, gypsies, bulls, wild horses, and rugged, taciturn, Hemingwayesque men. Many of the houses here are ranches, often long, low dwellings with adjoining stables and corrals. Stretching out over marsh and plains as far as the eye can see, the Mas de Cacherel, home of the old Provençal Colomb de Daunant family, is a classic example of a Camarguais ranch. Thick white plaster and stone walls enclose low, modestly proportioned rooms, keeping the interior unusually cool, considering the baking temperatures outside. Two other design elements geared to maintaining a cool interior are the tiles

The front entrance to the Mas de Cacherel is a small, vertically planked doorway flanked by enormous bushes of rosemary, above. The door and shutters are painted very pale gray to contrast, but just slightly, with the bright white exterior walls. The sun-bleached skull of a bull adorns a doorway, left—a Camarguais touch reminiscent of a Georgia O'Keeffe painting.

An assortment of wicker and rattan chairs remains empty until after sunset, when temperatures have finally cooled down enough for alfresco cocktails.

One of Madame Colomb de Daunant's specialties is a Provençal tomato juice cocktail made by macerating sliced lemons and a handful of fresh mint in a pitcher of tomato juice for about three hours; alone or spiked with gin or vodka, it's an extremely refreshing hot-weather aperitif.

covering all floors and some walls, and the small, widely spaced windows.

Beamed ceilings, tiles, regional furniture, and other characteristically Provençal elements meld harmoniously with the Wild West trappings of cowboy country, such as the surprising and dramatic glassed-in *sellerie,* or tack room, right off the living room, or Denis Colomb de Daunant's collection of firearms hung among the lithographs on the living room wall. Attached to the rear of the main residence is a *maison de gardian,* a ranch hand's tiny dwelling with its own spare charm. Although the overriding spirit of the ranch is direct and masculine, with few apparent flights of fancy, not everything is grounded and macho *chez* Cacherel. Flocks of skittish, white fantail doves swooping overhead, perching on rooftops, or surveying the landscape from their distinctive, enamel-tiled dovecote, add a delicate, almost ephemeral beauty in direct counterpoint to the dominant ruggedness of the *mas.*

Hanging from a ceiling beam in the kitchen, right, are hot peppers, herbs, and garlic. Open storage areas under the sink and next to the stove are simply covered by red-checked curtains. By the kitchen window, left, a 19th-century *pétrin* from Arles displays local faïence and a collection of sapphire blue apothecary bottles.

A 19th-century *horloge provençal,* or Provençal pendulum clock, keeps time by a kitchen door. The bread-dough bull's head above the door is a whimsical wall decoration in the spirit of the Camargue.

Set into the large living room fireplace, today rarely used, is a large 18th-century *farinière,* or flour box, to the left, and a pair of massive, locally made wrought-iron andirons, designed to hold pots.

In the living room next to the glass window of the *sellerie* is a Louis XV Provençal writing table. The floor of medallion-shaped terra-cotta tiles, bordered by strips of blue-and-white faïence tiles, was designed by Monsieur Colomb de Daunant.

The long dining table in the living room is tiled, like one in the kitchen, in blue-and-white tiles laid by Denis Colomb de Daunant. Decorating the walls of the long, low room is an eclectic mix of firearms, bull's horns, and antique lithographs.

In the *petit salon,* or small sitting room off the living room, all the furniture, such as these two chairs and the round, hand-painted turn-of-the-century table, are scaled down in size to accommodate the room's diminutive proportions. The hand-painted screen, created around 1925 by a regional artist, depicts a religious scene with the black gypsy Madonna, Sarah, in the boat.

In the center of the house, right off the living room, a glassed-in *sellerie,* or tack room, dramatically displays a family collection of saddles, bits, and prize ribbons.

In a daughter's
bedroom, which looks
out on the *marais,* or
marshes, twenty feet
away, a collection of
straw hats from her
travels covers the walls.
A 19th-century
encoignure, or corner
cabinet, sits across the
room from her bed. An
Empire-style bed serves
as a sofa.

The bed is a very simple
19th-century *litoche.*
The fabrics of the
curtains and the
bedspreads are early
1950s copies of the
classic 18th- and 19th-
century fabrics from
Jouy.

Behind the *mas,* a stylish *colombier* with a green enamel tile border and a canal tile roof is home to a large, lively flock of pure white fantail doves.

Attached to the back of the *mas* is the simple, two-room house of the *gardian,* or ranch hand.

When the white horses of the Camargue are born, they are black like this young colt drinking in the *marais* next to the *mas.*

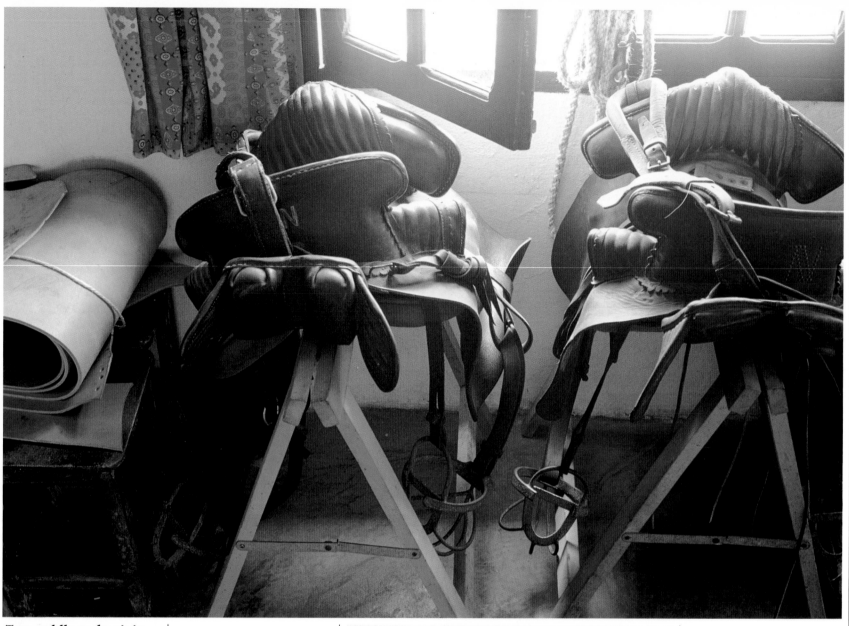

Two saddle racks sit in the living area of the *gardian*'s house.

Bulls roam throughout the Camargue, such as this pair on a plain near the Mas de Cacherel.

The living area of the *gardian*'s residence is furnished with the barest necessities—a table (covered by a plastic-coated Souleiado fabric), chairs, and a sofa bed.

One of Denis Colomb de Daunant's prize stallions peers out of his stall at visitors.

PROVENÇAL GARDENS

The distinctive gardens of Provence might be described most succinctly as patches and pots of brilliance. Bursts of startling, vivid color punctuate windowsills, doorways, outdoor stairways, backyard paths, poolside embankments, and no longer functioning wells. Because cultivable soil is precious in Provence and water is scarce, the best land is given over to edible or aromatic crops. Flowers, which no true Provençal

An old painted barrel, top left, a small volcanic boulder, top right, a large pottery urn, bottom left, and geraniums in a multitude of hues accent the garden of Marcel Perret in the small, shady town of Maussane. At a *mas* in Mouriès, bottom right, an urn of geraniums on a stone pedestal is camouflaged by a mound of ivy trained around it.

could live without, long ago found their proper place close to the house in urns, pots, and sundry other containers of all sizes and shapes. Small rock gardens are not uncommon, but they are not nearly as ubiquitous as the striking floral displays contained in tightly clustered pots.

The floral motifs in fabric and furniture are only one reflection of the Provençal passion for all manner of flowering plants. Roses, eglantines, acacias, marguerites, laurel, jasmine, petunias, chrysanthemums, lavender, and, of course, hearty geraniums bloom in a fragrant carnival of colors from Menton to Moustiers to Saintes-Maries-de-la-Mer. They flower almost all year round, except during the chilly, windy winter months. Most of them must be lovingly cared for, protected against the mistral, and lavished with water against the parching sun of the Provençal summer.

Early in this century, terraced gardens were à la mode in parts of Provence, but most now have grown wild and unkempt, the châteaux or villas they were attached to rented seasonally or abandoned totally. Their designs, though, were carefully thought out and implemented. On the first level, closest to the house, were the formal flower gardens with roses, mimosas, zinnias, chrysanthemums, and other small flowering plants. The next level, three or four steps below, usually held neat rows of lemon and almond trees planted over a much larger expanse of land. On the third level, another few steps down, low, clipped shrubs were arranged with geometric precision, while the lowest level, farthest away from the house, was most often a small vineyard.

Although today potted gardens have replaced terraced ones, the land is no less colorful for it. Almost everywhere you turn in Provence, on city streets or along country paths, at stately châteaux or by humble *mas,* your eye will almost certainly come to rest on a flower.

Pots of pink and red geraniums line the sill atop a butcher's shop in the old quarter of Saint-Rémy, the site of a former stove and cauldron works.

An old wine barrel holds a flourishing hydrangea bush by a back stairway at the Château de Fontarèches, left; farther along the same wall, a lemon tree fills a terracotta urn, right.

A huge terra-cotta pot adorned with ram's heads serves as a planter on a terrace in Le Paradou.

Outside Monsieur Paulet's small, quaint house, clustered pots of flowers surround the ochre walls.

Zinnias, marigolds, and marguerites are among the hearty flowers that populate Provençal gardens.

In the small rock garden in Le Paradou of Monsieur Paulet, left, flowers planted in the ground vie for space with pots of geraniums and assorted succulents, right.

193

An abundance of geraniums overflows two 19th-century urns outside the Château de Barbentane.

A troupe of terra-cotta pots holding a variety of flowering plants, left, is stationed atop a stone wall dividing the back lawn of the Château de Fontarèches.

Pots of geraniums punctuate a lush wall of ivy in Uzès and brighten a nearby stone well, right.

A gnarled oriental plane tree, left, on the grounds of the Château de Barbentane is more than 200 years old.

Within a tranquil niche, right, geraniums grow out of a typically Provençal green pottery urn.

The Marquis de Barbentane recently designed a pool and an *orangerie*, or greenhouse, in the 19th-century style of a large fountain and reflecting pool at the entrance to his château. The *orangerie*'s iron-framed panes of glass enhance a tranquil view of the terrace and pool.

Two large clumps of spider chrysanthemums flank the steps to the *orangerie*, which houses a variety of potted plants in various stages of development.

Maintaining a richly diverse and extravagantly colorful garden throughout a Provençal summer requires, in addition to almost constant attention, enormous quantities of water.

A large *potager,* or vegetable garden, in Mouriès, above, is brightly bordered by tall flowers. A lavishly blossomed crepe myrtle, left, is the centerpiece of a lush garden in Mouriès.

A wrought-iron trellis, left, is the entrance to the garden.

Two tall cypresses, above, mark the beginning of the *allée* through the vegetable garden toward the house in Mouriès. A sapling planted in an ancient grinding wheel, left, makes an intriguing sculptural form along a garden path.

Across the road from the *mas*, a small stone house, left, nearly 200 years old encloses a large well.

In the shade of two tall plane trees in Mouriès, white wrought-iron garden furniture offers cool respite.

FRENCH COUNTRY
ADAPTATIONS

 The entrancing physical presence of the French countryside—the sunlight, the scent, the wind, the roll of the land—is unique and cannot be re-created or transplanted; you simply have to be there to experience it. But the *style* of the French countryside, the colors, the fabrics, the furniture, the decorative accents, the way the French mix the elements together, can transcend its regional sources, and in the decorative sense comprises a bountiful, movable feast. We found aspects of the

French country look in areas as diverse as Beverly Hills, California; Woodstock, New York; and Beaumont, Texas. And the ways in which people use French country components, from tiles to tureens to armoires, are astounding in their diversity. There is the diminutive, sun-filled cottage in Carmel, where the simple, joyful combination of furniture, fabrics, and tile perhaps best expresses the transcendent warmth and charm of provincial France; the Greenwich Village town house with a French country kitchen that belies any hint of the city that is just outside the window; the farm in Woodstock, New York, that combines elements of French and American country styles so skillfully that the two seem to derive from a single design source; and the home near Los Angeles where a rich collection of provincial furniture sets off an ambiance that is pure California.

In our travels and extensive scouting throughout the United States and on a brief stop in Paris, we discovered that rather than try to re-create pure French country settings, where every item and element originates from provincial France, most devotees of the French country look adapt aspects of the style to complement existing décors. What we found striking was how well the components worked in other than French country environments, dressed up or down in settings that range from starkly contemporary to oriental to American country.

In this section of the book, we take a room-by-room look at French country fabrics, furniture, tiles, and accents as they are used far removed from their source. Here, as we mentioned in our Introduction, elements from many provinces are featured, not exclusively Provence; items that we describe as "provincial," such as farm tables, originated and can be found in any one of several regions of France. Adapted with the imagination and warmth that characterizes the style at its source, the elements of the French country look impart a distinction and a charm to their surroundings, whether they are used as simply as the Provençal fabric covering a crib bumper, or as imposingly as the rare and majestic armoire reigning over a spacious city living room.

Set between two fan-topped French doors in a New Orleans living room is a Louis XV–style 19th-century *canapé* upholstered in Provençal fabric.

LIVING ROOMS

In most homes the living room is the showcase of the house, and the living rooms we feature are no exception. French country style appears here in a variety of guises—as the room's dominant theme, as an element in an eclectic mix of styles, or as the key accent that catches the eye and makes the difference.

In Virginia Campbell's Monterey coast cottage built in the 1920s, a French country theme is carried through in variations of red, white, and blue. To the right of the fireplace a provincial farm table of mixed woods holds an assortment of *objets*. A Louis XVI *bonne femme* armchair sits nearby.

A small windowsill still life in red, white, and blue echoes the color scheme of the room.

A set of white-and-blue Italian fireplace tiles that beautifully complements the French provincial theme leans against a mantelpiece, creating an attractive although unattached façade. On the mantelpiece rest carved French and Italian lambs.

In a cozy country sitting room in Connecticut, a provincial 18th-century steel campaign bed is now a sofa with a mattress covered with a lively Provençal cotton print (repeated in the curtains and the tablecloth) and an assortment of throw pillows. In the foreground are two comfortable 18th-century Voltaire armchairs. An American rag rug covers the widely planked floor.

A subdued mixture of Provençal fabrics and patterns marks the Pierre Deux country house living room in rural Connecticut. The chair to the left is an 18th-century Normandy side chair; the armchair to the right is a 17th-century *fauteuil de théâtre*. The 18th-century desk from Normandy is placed on a diagonal facing into the room to avoid giving the room a too-symmetrical look.

In Sandy Duncan's upstate New York farmhouse retreat, the flavors of French and American country blend harmoniously. Pillows covered in Souleiado fabrics pick up the colors in the white wicker furniture, the rag rug, and the fan-motif quilt on the wall, sewn by Miss Duncan's grandmother.

The centerpiece of a small Carmel, California, living room, a 19th-century provincial armoire with its doors reversed functions as a copiously filled display cabinet.

The focal point of a formal living room in San Francisco is a beautiful 18th-century Loire Valley *buffet à deux corps* in walnut, left. Next to the fireplace, topped by a gilt Regency mirror with grape clusters, is a carefully maintained Louis XVI walnut commode created in Nice, above.

A stand designed to hold a cool pitcher of water, this Directoire *rafraichissoir* is used as an end table in a Woodside, California, living room.

Holding the television set in a large home in Beaumont, Texas, is an early 19th-century oak armoire from Normandy with its doors attached inside out.

A provincial table converted from a small bench serves as a coffee table in the Woodside living room.

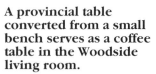

In the small living room of Tammy Grimes' New York pied-à-terre, a late 19th-century wine-tasting table from Champagne, accompanied by polished-steel folding French park chairs, serves as a spot for informal dining.

This slightly strange view of a Dallas living room includes an elegant little 18th-century *meuble de maîtrise* in the foreground, which is only a foot and a half high. The tall 18th-century pendulum clock in the background is a Saint Nicholas from Normandy.

In the living room of Helen Gurley Brown's New York apartment, a rare 18th-century Provençal armoire with spectacular detailing dominates the oriental fabrics and accessories.

Below the cornice of the armoire, an unusual carving of a fox and a stork was inspired by a fable by La Fontaine.

DINING ROOMS

A French country feeling comes across strongly in these diverse rooms, even though most are a mixture of two or more styles. In a couple of instances, the flower-sprigged walls of a sun-filled room set the provincial mood and highlight the French pieces; in others, it is the furniture itself that carries the impression. Even the small addition of provincial soup tureens can key the style.

A round 19th-century table from Champagne, left, is surrounded by four provincial Louis XVI chairs in the floral, feminine breakfast room of Mrs. Ross Bagdasarian in Los Angeles.

Strikingly unique, the beamed dining room of a Carmel estate, above, accommodates a huge 17th-century oak convent table surrounded by late 19th-century Provençal side chairs. At the end of the room is an 18th-century *buffet à deux corps* in oak from the Île de France. Stretched between the windows is an 18th-century Provençal *banquette,* left, with cushions made from original 18th-century hand-blocked *indienne* fabrics.

A provincial dessert table, above, from Ille-et-Vilaine sits against a dining room wall in a contemporary Woodstock, New York, weekend home.

The dining room of a town house on New York's East Side maintains a French flavor with a 19th-century *dressoir,* or sideboard, from Ille-et-Vilaine, left.

223

In a juxtaposition between provincial and avant-garde, an 18th-century *commode provençal* is flanked by bentwood Prague chairs and sits below a sculpture by Herbert Creecy in the New York dining room of Tim and Nina Zagat.

In the Beverly Hills dining room of Ross Bagdasarian, Jr., and his wife, decorator Janice Karman, a 19th-century French farm table is surrounded by American Windsor chairs; seat cushions, not shown, are made from Provençal print fabric. The elaborate 18th-century armoire with glass-paneled doors is from Normandy.

The beamed dining room of the Pierre Deux home in rural Connecticut is furnished rustically with an 18th-century Provençal buffet in walnut on the right wall, early 19th-century provincial chairs, and a 19th-century Ille-et-Vilaine *dressoir*. The fabrics of the curtains, seat cushions, napkins, and tablecloth liner are all Provençal cottons.

A hand-painted French provincial screen created about 1829 and a painted 18th-century blue-and-white buffet from the Île-de-France region lend a romantic air to a small dining room on Telegraph Hill in San Francisco.

A set of three 18th-century Luneville tureens adds a graceful French touch to the modern, glass-enclosed dining porch of a Sonoma country estate in California.

BEDROOMS

Provincial style, with its romantic spirit and emphasis on comfort, can be beautifully adapted to the bedroom. Delicate curtains of handworked lace, bedspreads of vibrant, graceful cotton prints, and armoires, chests, and chairs of richly toned wood together create a welcoming mood that imparts a strong sense of *bien-être,* or well-being.

Cathy Kincaid, a Dallas decorator and a mother enamored of French Provençal prints, outfitted her new baby's room, right, almost entirely in Souleiado fabrics and wallpaper; the quilt on the wall is American but softly complements the Provençal patterns. A lively and unusual crib bumper was created from a Souleiado border print.

A feminine blue-and-white bedroom in San Francisco includes a French-dressed bed with a modified canopy in Brunschwig fabric, above, and a dainty, airy white eyelet coverlet and matching square pillow shams. An 18th-century Hautes-Alpes buffet in wild cherry, left, serves as a dresser.

Handworked lace curtains, below, created in northern Provence about 1880, cover a San Francisco bedroom window.

A romantic and feminine bedroom in Los Angeles includes a 19th-century *table basculante*, or tilt-top table, from Champagne, to the right of the bed; floral-splashed French pillowcases and the blanket cover are by Porthault.

233

In the masculine, putty-colored bedroom of Robert Grabow in Carmel, California, right, a small provincial cherrywood armoire adds warmth to the room's understated décor and oriental accents.

A *banquette* seat with Provençal print cushions and assorted throw pillows and a canopy bed hung with Provençal fabric, above, add a fresh French country look to a bedroom in suburban Dallas.

Original *toile de Jouy* fabric cushions cover an 18th-century *bonne femme* armchair, left; next to the armchair is an 18th-century *table de chevet,* or bedside table.

In a bedroom in Los Angeles, above, a Louis XVI *fauteuil* holds part of its inhabitant's collection of dolls. Next to the chair is an 18th-century Provençal writing table displaying, among other objects, a Provençal *meuble de maitrise*—an apprentice cabinetmaker's crafts-manship project. Another, larger *meuble de maître* is under the table.

Upstairs in the Greenwich Village town house of Wayne and Lydie Marshall, a walnut armchair of the Directoire period and a Louis XVI provincial walnut commode, left, add to the French flavor of the bedroom; on the floor is a blue-and-white Chinese rug. A small foyer with an early 19th-century armoirette from Anjou leads into the bedroom, where the Empire bed is covered with an American quilt, below.

A simple country bedroom in rural Connecticut, above, has walls covered with a blue-and-white Provençal print fabric; assorted Provençal cotton throw pillows add a dash of color to the white bedcovers. The desk chair is a Restoration *fauteuil* from Provence; the 18th-century chest to the right of the desk is from Ille-et-Vilaine.

Provincial lace curtains hung from wooden rings and a provincial 19th-century armoire add a quaint and cozy French look to Tammy Grimes' small bedroom in her New York pied-à-terre, below.

KITCHENS

The heart of the home is perhaps the best of all rooms to endow with French country flair, for it is here at the source of family sustenance that domestic life and the warmth and easygoing charm of provincial style are most in harmony. From the kitchen of a narrow city apartment in Paris to that of a plantation-style house in Texas, the unique elements of the French country look create rooms that are special, personal, and *sympathique.*

A strong French flavor emanates from the kitchen of Mr. and Mrs. Will Ohmstede's plantation-style house in Beaumont, Texas. Behind the central work island, folding doors open onto the dining room so that during informal dinners guests can enjoy the cozy provincial ambiance of the kitchen. Flooring of large, rectangular terra-cotta tiles extends throughout the entire first floor of the house.

Heavy French copperware pots and pans, as well as wicker and wire baskets and a braid of garlic, hang from a suspended pot rack above the stove in the Ohmstede kitchen.

A Directoire monastery table abuts an inset 19th-century glass cupboard with a clock from Bresse in the former pantry of an estate in Carmel, above; the old hexagonal terra-cotta tiles were brought over from Provence.

An 18th-century walnut *bonnetière*, or cabinet designed to hold bonnets, dominates the small kitchen of the Carmel estate, below.

The Ohmstede's kitchen table, left, set in a glassed-in eating nook with two French-style bakers' racks, is a 19th-century Provençal drop-leaf in walnut. The cushions on the 19th-century provincial chairs are in Provençal print cotton fabric, as are the small lampshades.

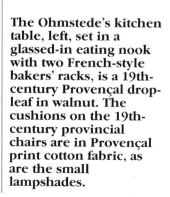

Adding visual interest as well as a work surface to the mixed-woods kitchen of Ross Bagdasarian, Jr., and Janice Karman in Beverly Hills, above, is an old French butcher's table.

Hanging like a mobile in the center of the kitchen of an estate in Carmel, below, is a provincial spoon holder.

In the dining area of Charleen Matoza's Carmel kitchen, left, a long 19th-century fruitwood farm table seats up to twelve guests; the provincial side chairs also date from the 19th century.

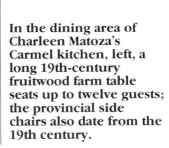

The small, sleek, modern kitchen of the Pierre Deux apartment in Paris includes a scaled-down early 19th-century marble-topped bistro table, left, set against the glossy pale gray wall. St. Germain faïence tiles with French revolutionary motifs run in back of the stove and sink, above.

A rustic collection of 19th-century Dordogne pots, above, is displayed on top of the cabinets in the Pierre Deux Paris apartment.

In a niche near the kitchen window in Wayne and Lydie Marshall's 19th-century Greenwich Village town house, below, is an 18th-century *garde-manger,* or food storage cabinet, from Brittany; on top are two old vinegar kegs purchased at French flea markets, right, in which Wayne Marshall makes his own vinegar, and two bottles in which he stores it.

Set for an alfresco dinner for four, a garden table in the New Orleans courtyard of Milton Melton and Stephen Scalia is covered with a vibrant floral tablecloth by Pierre Frey. Balloon-patterned soup dishes are by the Atelier de Ségriès in Moustiers; the pewter liners are Portuguese. Simon Pearce created the long-stemmed wineglasses.

TABLE SETTINGS

With faïence, a tablecloth, and glassware from the French provinces, a simple table takes on a jaunty air of Gallic *esprit.* Here are just a few examples of French country-style tables to set anywhere. Whether it's a Bastille Day celebration with charcuterie, cheeses, salads, and Beaujolais overlooking the skyline of New York, a spring breakfast of croissants and café au lait in New Orleans, or an informal supper of fried chicken, corn bread, and iced tea in your own backyard, a provincial table setting marks the repast as special and provides a delectable complement to the food.

A marble-topped Victorian table flanked by two French park chairs holds Provençal print place mats, Simon Pearce provincial-style glassware, and an 18th-century-style French pewter tureen in preparation for an outdoor buffet in a New Orleans courtyard.

On a balcony in New Orleans' French Quarter, a small round table is set for breakfast for two. A Souleiado Baumanière tablecloth picks up the colors of the local greenery and the roof across the way. The pink-and-white faïence is from Moustiers; the provincial-style glassware is by Simon Pearce.

The long table in Lydie Marshall's kitchen, scene of her "A la Bonne Cocotte" cooking school, is prepared for a Sunday supper *à quatre*. The porcelain, set over Provençal cotton place mats, is from Gien; the Gien tureen rests on a *scourtin*, or Provençal hemp olive-oil filter. The carafe and wineglasses are 19th-century French crystal.

A Bastille Day celebration is laid out high above the New York skyline in photographer Susan Wood's Fifth Avenue apartment, right. Provençal cotton fabric in a red, white, and blue print covers the long table. Faïence plates with French revolutionary symbols and slogans, below, are by St. Germain. The red, white, and blue theme is carried through in the chunky candles and the flowers.

In Sam Watters' diminutive upstate New York country house, a small round table is set for an intimate late-afternoon Christmas dinner, left. Tablecloths and napkins were created from a variety of red, green, and white Souleiado prints. The faïence is the new Chinese Dancers pattern from the Atelier de Ségriès in Moustiers. Crystal de Sèvres produces the pewter-stemmed glassware. A pair of little *santons* decorates each place setting.

VIGNETTES

Nooks, niches, and corners are chosen spots in many homes for adding a French country accent. Using provincial pieces this way gives a room an element of the unexpected. Another point to consider is that if you have only one or two provincial treasures—an 18th-century soup tureen or a 19th-century buffet—you might show them off to their best advantage in unusual surroundings where they catch and hold the eye. Here we offer a pastiche of *vignettes,* or short takes, on intriguing manifestations of French country style.

An early 19th-century walnut nightstand serves as a telephone table in the foyer of a Carmel, California, estate, left; the chair is an 18th-century *fauteuil à la bonne femme*.

A 19th-century oak *buffet-vaisselier* from Normandy, above, has been trimmed to half its original depth to serve as an attractive, unusual, and practical bar in the Houston home of Charles Sanders and Ed Harris.

An 18th-century Île-de-France commode in walnut, below, is among the fine collection of French antique furniture that fills an elegant lemon-yellow living room near Los Angeles.

Seen from a doorway in Geoffrey Beene's Long Island home, right, is a Mediterranean Directoire wrought-iron chair next to a mirror set in an 18th-century French gilt frame; reflected in the mirror is a *style moderne* sculpture of bathers placed by a window in a guest bathroom.

The graceful lines of a small russet-toned Louis XV Provençal table, left, show to advantage in Geoffrey Beene's elegant vestibule.

Set between two kitchen closet doors in Mr. Beene's home, a late 18th-century Provençal table with painted latticework, above, is used as a telephone table.

A graceful 19th-century French cast-iron door knocker, right, is now attached to a vertically planked door in New Orleans' French Quarter.

In an English-French play on words, a Carmel, California, pool house, left, is also a *poule* house with its large collection of French hens. Rustic turn-of-the-century chairs and a *banquette* painted white provide informal seating. In the background is a large 19th-century French baker's rack; French bistro mirrors hang on the wall.

A soupçon of France is added to a tiny balcony overlooking San Francisco Bay by a small turn-of-the-century French garden table and folding garden chairs, above, both painted green to harmonize with the potted plants.

Stationed by the doorway leading onto a small balcony in Carmel, a Souleiado-clad doll sits on an exact reproduction of a Louis XVI *chaise à la gerbe,* or Provençal side chair, right. On the balcony itself a carved redwood garden chair is enlivened by a Provençal print cushion.

Set out on the veranda of a Sonoma Valley estate, right, is an 18th-century *fleuri*-style *bonne femme* armchair in walnut, created in Arles.

Tucked into a niche in the hallway of a Los Angeles home is a small 18th-century Provençal table, left, from Arles set below a glass-front étagère of the same period and place. The soup tureen is 18th-century faïence from Marseilles.

Complementing the graceful lines of a French Art Deco bronze in a New York apartment is a Louis Philippe provincial armchair, below, upholstered in a linen and cotton blend by Knoll.

A 19th-century French butcher's table with a wrought-iron and brass base, right, functions as a bar in the atrium of a San Francisco home.

In a Beverly Hills study, the Provençal print fabric on an overstuffed armchair, above, matches that on the fabric-covered miniblinds.

Combining the sleekly modern with the charmingly provincial, Tim and Nina Zagat paired a Breuer "Wassily" chair with a 19th-century Alsatian ceramic-tiled stove, right, in the foyer of their New York apartment.

A 19th-century farm table from Normandy in cherry, below, is surrounded by plants in a sunny Los Angeles living room.

DIRECTORY

A GUIDE TO FRENCH COUNTRY SOURCES

Many products of the French countryside are widely available in the United States, as well as throughout France. In this directory we offer an overview of where you can obtain furniture, fabrics, faïence, tiles, and a broad range of decorative accessories similar to the ones featured in this book. We cover sources both in the United States and, for those of you who will be traveling in Europe or who have the patience for lengthy transatlantic mail-order transactions, in France and England. In the U.S. section we also include a listing of decorators adept at creating a French country look. Some sources are exclusively wholesale or "to the trade only," which means that purchases usually have to be made through a decorator; in these cases a (W) appears at the end of the listing. Keep in mind that, in addition to the specialized sources covered, many major department stores, such as Bloomingdale's, Macy's, Gump's, Neiman-Marcus, Bullock's, Marshall Field, and large home stores such as Conran's regularly stock French country products. Our directory is far from exhaustive, but it does provide a good base for anyone scouting at home or abroad for provincial furnishings, both antique and new. Listings, as we go to press, are accurate and up to date.

IN THE UNITED STATES
ANTIQUE FURNITURE

Unless a particular specialty is noted, the antiques dealers listed here carry a variety of provincial French furniture. Most welcome special requests from collectors seeking pieces from a certain region or period and will keep an eye out for them during their buying trips.

NORTHEAST/ MID-ATLANTIC

Antan Antiques Ltd.
Yellow Monkey Village
Rte. 35
Cross River, NY 10518
(914) 763-5115

Antiques International
53 East 10th St.
New York, NY 10003
(212) 777-4360 (W)

Blossom Cove
655 Broad St.
Shrewsbury, NY 07701
(201) 747-6550

Le Cadet de Gascogne
1021 Lexington Ave.
New York, NY 10021
(212) 744-5925

Chrystian Aubusson, Inc.
969 Third Ave.
New York, NY 10022
(212) 755-2432

George I. Gravert
122 Charles St.
Boston, MA 02108
(617) 227-1593

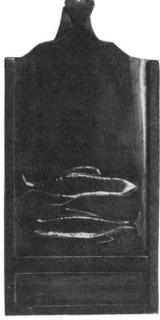

Hamilton Hyre
413 Bleecker St.
New York, NY 10014
(212) 989-4509
Specializing in faux bamboo

Howard Kaplan's French Country Store
35 East 10th St.
New York, NY 10003
(212) 674-1000
Country furniture and household items (W)

James Graftstein
236 East 60th St.
New York, NY 10022
(212) 754-1290

Jean-Paul Beaujard
209 East 76th St.
New York, NY 10021
(212) 249-3790
Napoleon III furniture

Maison Jean-François, Inc.
67 East 11th St.
New York, NY 10003
(212) 674-2140 (W)

Marcoz
177 Newbury St.
Boston, MA 02116
(617) 262-0780

Mendelsohn Galleries
6826 Wisconsin Ave.
Chevy Chase, MD 20815
(301) 656-2766

Miller & Arney Antiques
1737 Wisconsin Ave. NW
Washington, DC 20007
(202) 338-2369

Old Versailles, Inc.
215 East 75th St.
New York, NY 10021
(212) 421-3663
18th-century furniture

Peter Mack Brown Antiques
1525 Wisconsin Ave. NW
Washington, DC 20007
(202) 338-8484
18th-century furniture

Pierre Deux Antiques
369 Bleecker St.
New York, NY 10014
(212) 243-7740

Les Trois Provinces
Church St.
New Preston, CT 06777
(203) 868-7961

SOUTH/ SOUTHWEST

Antiques and Interiors
1138 Royal St.
New Orleans, LA 70116

Bradley on the Plaza
6730 Snider Plaza
Dallas, TX 75205
(204) 363-3252

Brian Stringer
2031 W. Alabama
Houston, TX 77098
(713) 526-7380

Bunny Davis Antiques
2269 Peachtree Rd. NE
Atlanta, GA 30305
(404) 351-1738

Camel Antiques
1000 E. Camelback Rd.
Phoenix, AZ 85014
(602) 277-0101

Le Chanteclaire
470 Mariposa St.
Beaumont, TX 77701
(713) 892-7862

E. C. Dicken
1505 Oak Lawn
Dallas, TX 75207
(214) 742-4801

Elaine Dixon Antiques
Omni
1601 Biscayne Blvd.
Miami, FL 33132
(305) 358-7234

The Elephant Foot
310 S. Olive
West Palm Beach, FL 33401
(305) 832-0170

French Antique Shop
225 Royal St.
New Orleans, LA 70116
(504) 524-9861

The Gables
3125 Piedmont Rd. NE
Atlanta, GA 30305
(404) 231-0734

Hayes-Leger Associates, Inc.
Atlanta Decorative
Arts Center
351 Peachtree Hills Ave. NE
Atlanta, GA 30305
(404) 233-7425

Henry Stern Antiques
329 Royal St.
New Orleans, LA 70116
(504) 522-8687

Lucky's Antiques
170 NE 40th St.
Miami, FL 33137
(305) 573-7788

Manheim Galleries
409 Royal St.
New Orleans, LA 70130
(504) 568-1901

The Market
4236 Oak Lawn
Dallas, TX 75219
(214) 528-9070

Orion Decorative Antiques
1628 Oak Lawn
Dallas, TX 75207
(214) 748-1177

Peter Lawrence Fine Antiques
234-A South County Rd.
Palm Beach, FL 33480
(305) 832-0227

Steven Ewing Antiques
2013 W. Gray
Houston, TX 77019
(713) 523-0394

Twery's Antiques
160 NE 40th St.
Miami, FL 33137
(305) 576-0564

Zante
2402 Bissonnet
Houston, TX 77006
(713) 522-9777

MIDWEST/WEST

A La Douce France
6919 La Jolla Blvd.
La Jolla, CA 92037
(714) 459-7026

Au Marché, Inc.
320 Ward Pkwy.
Kansas City, MO 64112
(816) 531-6633

Baldacchino
919 N. La Cienega Blvd.
Los Angeles, CA 90069
(213) 657-6810

Connoisseur
910 Linden
Winnetka, IL 60093
(312) 446-1366

David Weatherford
133 14th Ave. E.
Seattle, WA 98102
(206) 329-6533

Don Badertscher Imports
716 N. La Cienega Blvd.
Los Angeles, CA 90069
(213) 655-6448
Turn-of-the-century furniture

The Dove Cote
1550 Tiburon Blvd.
Belevedere, CA 94920
(415) 435-9120

La Fille du Roi
P.O. Box 1873
Carmel, CA 93921
(408) 625-3313

The French Connection
29 N. Santa Cruz Ave.
Los Gatos, CA 95030
(408) 354-2232

Globe Antiques
529 Pine St.
Seattle, WA 98101
(206) 682-1420

G. R. Durenberger
31431 Cam. Capistrano
San Juan Capistrano, CA 92675
(714) 493-1283

John J. Nelson Antiques & Accessories
8472 Melrose Pl.
Los Angeles, CA 90069
(213) 652-2103

Licorne
8432 Melrose Pl.
Los Angeles, CA 90069
(213) 852-4765
12th- through 20th-century furniture

La Maison Française Antiques
8420 Melrose Pl.
Los Angeles, CA 90069
(213) 653-6534
15th- to early 19th-century furniture

Mike Bell, Inc.
220 W. Kinzie
Chicago, IL 60610
(312) 644-6848

La Remise de Soleil
704 Samson St.
San Francisco, CA 94111
(415) 434-0657

Sebree Galleries
301 E. 55th St.
Kansas City, MO 64113
(816) 333-3387

Sixth Avenue Antiques
1330 6th Ave.
Seattle, WA 98101
(206) 622-1110

Speirs-Laughlin Antiques
8461 Melrose Pl.
Los Angeles, CA 90069
(213) 653-4600

Sugar Loaf
160 Sir Francis Drake Blvd.
San Anselmo, CA 94960
(415) 457-1999

FRENCH FABRICS AND WALL COVERINGS

These sources offer a variety of French fabrics and/or wall coverings in provincial styles. Stores selling Souleiado *provençal* cotton prints appear under separate listings that follow.

A. B. Closson & Co.
401 Race St.
Cincinnati, OH 45202
(513) 762-5500

Boussac of France
979 Third Ave.
New York, NY 10022
(212) 421-0534 (W)

Brunschwig & Fils
979 Third Ave.
New York, NY 10022
(212) 838-7878 (W)

Clarence House
40 East 57th St.
New York, NY 10022
(212) 752-2890 (W)

La France Imports, Inc.
2008 Sepulveda Blvd.
Los Angeles, CA 90025
(213) 478-6009

Laura Ashley
714 Madison Ave.
New York, NY 10021
(212) 371-0606

Maison de Campagne, Inc.
Station Square
Pittsburgh, PA 15219
(412) 765-0587
Boussac of France fabrics

Manuel Canovas, Inc.
979 Third Ave.
New York, NY 10022
(212) 688-5611
Silks, cottons (W)

Rose Cumming
232 East 59th St.
New York, NY 10022
(212) 758-1029
Specializing in chintz (W)

St.-Rémy L'Herbier de Provence
156 East 64th St.
New York, NY 10021
(212) 759-8240

Schumacher, Inc.
979 Third Ave.
New York, NY 10022
(212) 644-5900
Jacquard weaves, tapestries (W)

Winfield Design Associates, Inc.
2690 Harrison St.
San Francisco, CA 94110
(415) 647-6787
Nobilis fabric and wall coverings (W)

Yves Gonnet
979 Third Ave.
New York, NY 10022
(212) 758-8220
Cotton prints, chintzes, and textured wools (W)

Zumsteg, Inc.
979 Third Ave.
New York, NY 10022
(212) 355-4010
19th-century design fabrics and wall coverings (W)

INTERIOR DECORATORS

The decorators mentioned here work in a variety of styles, according to client tastes and needs, but are particularly skilled in both implementing a total French country theme or adapting French country accents to another design style.

NORTHEAST/ MID-ATLANTIC

Alexandra Stoddard
1125 Park Ave.
New York, NY 10028
(212) 289-0084

Antony Childs, Inc.
1670 Wisconsin Ave. NW
Washington, DC 20007
(202) 337-1100

Barbara Halperin
45 E. 66th St.
New York, NY 10021
(212) 628-3012

Bennett & Judy Weinstock
2026 Delancey Place
Philadelphia, PA 19105
(215) 545-3206

Bierly-Drake Assoc., Inc.
172 Newbury St.
Boston, MA 02116
(617) 247-0081

Cooper and French Interior Design
112 Williams St.
Newport, RI 02840
(401) 846-4454

David Laurence Roth
40 East 69th Street
New York, NY 10021
(212) 879-8100

Denning and Fourcade
125 East 73rd St.
New York, NY 10021
(212) 759-1969

Donghia and Associates
315 East 62nd St.
New York, NY 10021
(212) 486-1167

Douglas Martin
1618 Pine St.
Philadelphia, PA 19146
(215) 735-8684

Easton and LaRocca, Inc.
323 East 58th St.
New York, NY 10022
(212) 838-5244

George Clarkson
117 East 57th St.
New York, NY 10022
(212) 759-7226

Georgina Fairholme
11 East 75th Street
New York, NY 10021
(212) 744-7993

Interior Impressions
8534 Connecticut Ave.
Chevy Chase, MD 20815
(301) 657-4490

Janine Chaneles
54 W. 74th St.
New York, NY 10023
(212) 724-5820

MAC II
121 East 81st Street
New York, NY 10021
(212) 249-4466

Jerome Manashaw
527 Madison Ave.
New York, NY 10022
(212) 838-8741

Kevin McNamara, Inc.
541 East 72nd St.
New York, NY 10021
(212) 861-0808

Mario Buatta
120 East 80th St.
New York, NY 10021
(212) 988-6811

Mark Hampton, Inc.
654 Madison Ave.
New York, NY 10021
(212) 753-4110

McMillen Inc.
155 East 56th St.
New York, NY 10022
(212) 753-6377

The Outlook
Mrs. Allison Loring
East Shore Rd.
Southport, ME 04576
(207) 633-4658

Parish-Hadley Associates
305 E. 63rd St.
New York, NY 10021
(212) 888-7979

Roach and Craven, Inc.
9 Willow St.
Boston, MA 02108
(617) 742-2080

Robert Kimberly Steever Kimberly
581 Hoyt St.
Darien, CT 06820

Richard Fitzgerald & Co., Inc.
7 Louisburg Sq.
Boston, MA 02108
(617) 742-1450

Susan Thorn
Cross River, NY 10518
(914) 763-5265

Thelma Turkel Interiors
7 Burgess Rd.
Scarsdale, NY 10583
(212) 734-1838

Thomas Fleming and Keith Irvine
19 East 57th St.
New York, NY 10022
(212) 888-6000

Unusual Interiors
410 E. Market St.
Charlottesville, VA 22901
(804) 293-9636

William Hodgins, Inc.
232 Clarendon St.
Boston, MA 02116
(617) 262-9538

SOUTH/ SOUTHWEST

Beverly Jacomini
2013C W. Gray
Houston, TX 77019
(713) 524-8224

Bremermann Designs
1530 Washington Ave.
New Orleans, LA 70130
(504) 891-6227

Cathy Kincaid Interiors
6315 Woodland
Dallas, TX 75225
(214) 373-0951

Dan Carithers
2499 Montview Drive NW
Atlanta, GA 30305
(404) 355-8661

Donna Vallone
Berkeley House Ltd.
6125 E. Indian School Rd.
Phoenix, AZ 85018
(602) 945-0966

Dorothy Aubinoe Griffith Assoc.
221 Aragon Ave.
Coral Gables, FL 33134
(305) 443-5550

Dyess Interiors, Inc.
1822 Upland Rd.
West Palm Beach, FL 33401
(305) 686-7096

Harris, Sanders Interior Designs
2800 Kirby Dr.
Houston, TX 77098
(713) 526-5114

Jane Wendel Interiors, Inc.
5 Via Mizner
Palm Beach, FL 33480
(305) 655-5440

Jenice Benton Interior Design
401 S. Mill Ave.
Temple, AZ 85281
(602) 967-3392

J. H. Armer Co.
6926 Main
Scottsdale, AZ 85251
(602) 947-2407

Linda Pasley Interiors
4509 Highland Dr.
Dallas, TX 75205
(214) 522-9781

Lucille Andrus
1309 Nashville Ave.
New Orleans, LA 70115
(504) 897-3242

Marcia Bland Brown Interiors
3702 Fairmont
Dallas, TX 75219
(214) 521-1129

Marie Warren Interiors
345 Peachtree Hills Ave. NE
Atlanta, GA 30305
(404) 231-0630

Martha Smith, Inc.
308 Peruvian Ave.
Palm Beach, FL 33480
(305) 833-1400

Mary Jane Hardwicke
900 NE 100th St.
Ocala, FL 32671
(904) 732-7275

Nina Sloss Interiors
6008 Magazine St.
New Orleans, LA 70118
(504) 895-7668

Odessa Lithgow
3841 NE Second Ave.
Miami, FL 33137
(305) 573-3223

Peter A. Lendrum, Assoc., Inc.
2920 E. Camelback Rd.
Phoenix, AZ 85016
(602) 955-2100

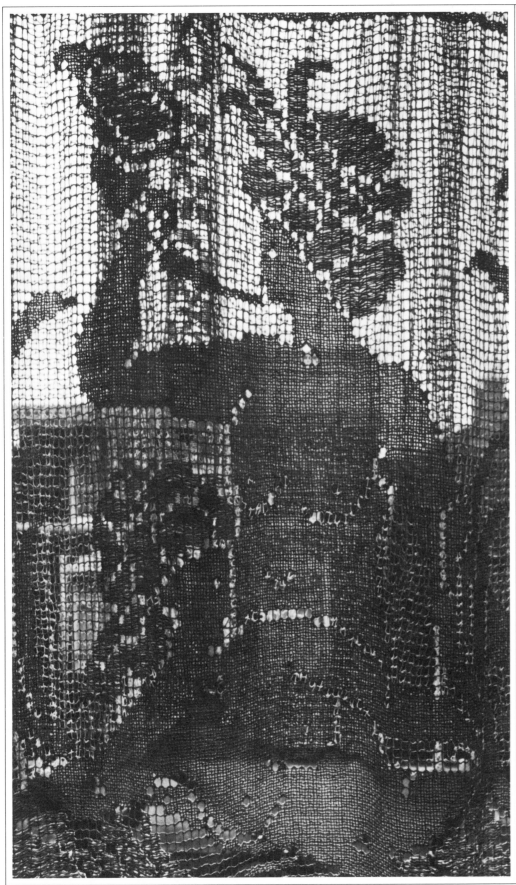

Phoebe L. Broido
44 Coconut Row
Palm Beach, FL 33480
(305) 655-0783

Robin Rodbell Interiors
116 Valley Rd. NW
Atlanta, GA 30305

MIDWEST/WEST

Bill Lane Assoc.
926 N. Orlando Ave.
Los Angeles, CA 90069
(213) 657-7890

Bruce Gregga Interiors, Inc.
1203 N. State Pkway.
Chicago, IL 60610
(312) 787-0017

Carol Knott Interiors
430 Greenbay Rd.
Kenilworth, IL 60043
(312) 256-6676

Cheryl Driven, Linda Floyd
The French Connection
29 N. Santa Cruz Ave.
Los Gatos, CA 95030
(408) 354-2232

Corinne Wiley
P.O. Box 513
Belvedere, CA 94920
(415) 435-3218

The Cottage
1338 E. Battlefield
Springfield, MO 65804
(417) 887-8779

Delsa Ham
Sugar Loaf
160 Sir Francis Drake Blvd.
San Anselmo, CA 94960
(415) 457-1999

Gayl Baddeley and Associates
510 South Sixth East St.
Salt Lake City, UT 84102
(801) 532-2435

Janet Polizzi, Inc.
8428 Melrose Pl.
Los Angeles, CA 90069
(213) 651-5177

Joe Haas
Au Marché
320 Ward Pkway.
Kansas City, MO 64112
(816) 531-6633

John Newcomb
P.O. Box 671
Carmel, CA 93921
(408) 624-9637

Marc T. Nielson
734 N. Old Sumac Road
Valparaiso, IN 46383
(219) 263-2631

**Maxine Smith
Celia Cleary
P'zazz**
9531 Hidder Valley
Beverly Hills, CA 90210
(213) 273-3437

Patricia Schlapp Interiors
13727 50th Ave. W
Edmonds, WA 98020
(206) 743-9078

**Le Poisson
Ken Poisson**
58 N. Santa Cruz Ave.
Los Gatos, CA 95030
(408) 354-9177

Ron Collier
P.O. Box 10719
Beverly Hills, CA 90210
(213) 278-5523

PIERRE DEUX STORES

The Pierre Deux shops offer an extensive selection of French country products, among them: Souleiado fabrics and accessories; Moustiers faïence; Saint Germain tableware; Ribeauville table linens; santons; and Marseilles soap and lavender sachets. The Pierre Deux shop at 369 Bleecker Street in New York City specializes in French country antiques, from faïence and small *objets* to ample armoires and *buffets-vaisseliers;* the shop at 870 Madison Avenue also offers a few antique pieces. The stores are listed here alphabetically by city.

Pierre Deux
111 W. Paces Ferry Rd. NW
Atlanta, GA 30305
(404) 262-7790

Pierre Deux
9700 Collins Ave.
Bal Harbour, FL 33154
(305) 864-1517

Pierre Deux
428 N. Rodeo Dr.
Beverly Hills, CA 90210
(213) 550-7265

Pierre Deux
111 Newbury St.
Boston, MA 02116
(617) 536-6364

Pierre Deux
P.O. Box 996
Carmel, CA 93921
(408) 624-8185

Pierre Deux
113 E. Oak St.
Chicago, IL 60611
(312) 642-9657

Pierre Deux
80 Highland Park Village
Dallas, TX 75205
(214) 528-5830

Pierre Deux
1800 S. Post Oak Blvd.
Houston, TX 77056
(713) 877-1313

Pierre Deux
519 Nichols Rd.
Kansas City, Mo 64112
(816) 753-2711

Pierre Deux
1144 Royal St.
New Orleans, LA 70116
(504) 522-4951

Pierre Deux
369 Bleecker St.
New York, NY 10014
(212) 243-7740

Pierre Deux
381 Bleecker St.
New York, NY 10014
(212) 675-4054

Pierre Deux
870 Madison Ave.
New York, NY 10021
(212) 570-9343

Pierre Deux
26 Via Mizner
Palm Beach, FL 33480
(305) 655-6810

Pierre Deux
532 Sutter St.
San Francisco, CA 94102
(415) 788-6380

Pierre Deux
6166 N. Scottsdale Rd.
Scottsdale, AZ 85253
(602) 948-0710

Pierre Deux
603 Union St.
Seattle, WA 98101
(206) 382-0745

Pierre Deux
Mazza Galleries
5300 Wisconsin Ave. NW
Washington, DC 20015
(202) 244-6226

Pierre Deux National
350 Bleecker St.
New York, NY 10014
(800) 221-4080
National Sales Office

SOULEIADO FABRICS/ PIERRE DEUX ACCESSORIES

The following stores carry a small selection of Souleiado fabrics as well as some French country accessories found in the Pierre Deux shops.

Bittners
236 Holiday Manor Center
Louisville, KY 40222
(502) 425-4555

China Closet
8712 Countryside Plaza
Omaha, NB 68114
(402) 393-7717

Cohoes Specialty Stores
43 Mohawk St.
Cohoes, NY 12047
(518) 237-0524

Design Alternatives
Titus Rd. at Rte. 47
Washington Depot, CT 06794
(203) 868-0325

The Eagle's Nest
Rte. 202
Morristown, NJ 07960
(201) 766-1372

Eaton's for the Collector
8 Adobe Ct.
Town & Country Village
Sacramento, CA 95821
(916) 485-2242

Eclectic Interiors
21 Babbit Rd.
Bedford Hills, NY 10507
(914) 241-0047

L'Esprit du Soleil
1067 South Gaylord St.
Denver, CO 80209
(303) 722-4791

The Fabric Gallery
731 South Aiken Ave.
Pittsburgh, PA 15232
(412) 682-0764

The Galloping Boutique
12 La Salle Rd.
West Hartford, CT 06107
(203) 521-7719

James Davis
400 Grove Park Rd.
Memphis, TN 38117
(901) 767-3855

Jeffrey Adams Antiques
401 Rodeo Rd.
Santa Fe, NM 87501
(505) 983-9797

June Kramer Inc.
1607 Colley Ave.
Norfolk, VA 23517
(804) 625-1211

LFK Limited
14 Post Rd. E.
Westport, CT 06880
(203) 227-0049

The Martin Glenn Corp.
dba Carpets by Stuart
2827 Oak St.
Eugene, OR 97405
(503) 485-8880

The Papery
15 East Washington St.
Middleburg, VA 22117
(703) 687-6423

Vitoch
45 Canterbury Rd.
Rochester, NY 14607
(716) 271-7760

TABLE LINENS/ BATH LINENS

These retailers, most of them linen specialists, offer an assortment of bed, bath, and table linens in provincial styles and prints. At New York's Cherchez you can occasionally find antique French lace-trimmed tablecloths, curtains, and sheets.

Cherchez
864 Lexington Ave.
New York, NY 10021
(212) 737-8215

Descamps
723 Madison Ave.
New York, NY 10021
(212) 355-2522

D. Porthault, Inc.
57 East 57th St.
New York, NY 10022
(212) 688-1661

Grand Central Mercantile Co.
222 First Ave. S.
Seattle, WA 98104
(206) 623-5389

Linen Designs, Inc.
473 Roger Williams Ave.
Highland Park, IL 60035
(312) 432-6126

The Staircase
8645 Sunset Blvd.
Los Angeles, CA 90069
(213) 652-7750

TABLEWARE

Faïence, plates, platters, bowls, and tureens from many regions of France, as well as various types of provincial glassware, candlesticks, and some flatware are available at the stores listed below.

Bazar Français of the Market, Inc.
666 Sixth Ave.
New York, NY 10010
(212) 243-6660

Delaware Interiors
337 East 55th St.
Kansas City, MO 64113
(816) 523-0330

Faire la Cuisine
8112 Melrose Ave.
Los Angeles, CA 90046
(213) 653-1464

Henri Bendel
10 West 57th St.
New York, NY 10019
(212) 247-1100

Made in France
2913 Ferndale
Houston, TX 70098
(713) 529-7949

La Maison en Soleil
317 Peruvian Ave.
Palm Beach, FL 33480
(305) 655-2938

The Market
4236 Oak Lawn
Dallas TX 75219
(214) 528-9070

The Mediterranean Shop
876 Madison Ave.
New York, NY 10021
(212) 879-3120

Mélangerie II Esplanade
150 Worth Ave.
Palm Beach, FL 33480
(305) 659-5119

The Pottery Barn
117 East 59th St.
New York, NY 10022
(212) 741-9132

La Ville du Soleil
556 Sutter St.
San Francisco, CA 94102
(415) 434-0657

Williams-Sonoma
5750 Hollis St.
Emeryville, CA 94608
(415) 652-1555
Catalogue available

TILES

Suppliers with a (W) following their listing, which sell wholesale only, will refer you to stores selling their products.

Auffray & Co.
146 East 56th St.
New York, NY 10022
(212) 753-3931
Terra-cotta tiles (W)

Cerabati/Monarch Tile Co.
P.O. Box 2401
San Angelo, TX 76901
(915) 655-9193
French tiles, glazed and encrusted mosaics (W)

Country Floors
8735 Melrose Ave.
Los Angeles, CA 90069
(213) 657-0510
Terra-cotta floor tiles, hand-painted wall tiles

Country Floors
94 NE 40th St.
Miami, FL 33137
(305) 576-0426

Country Floors
300 E. 61st St.
New York, NY 10021
(212) 758-7414

Country Floors
1706 Locust St.
Philadelphia, PA 19103
(215) 545-1040

French Brown Floors
707 Greenville Ave.
Dallas, TX 75231
(214) 363-4341

International Materials of Design
4585 Indian Creek Pkwy.
Overland Park, KS 66207
(913) 383-3383

Sunray Ceramics, Inc.
1507 Rand Rd.
Des Plaines, IL 60016
(312) 635-6300
Cerabati floor and wall tiles (W)

IN FRANCE

ANTIQUE FURNITURE

This listing of dealers barely scratches the surface of the French antiques world. The very best, most comprehensive, and most up-to-date listing of French antiques dealers is the *Guide Emer,* published yearly and widely available in bookstores throughout France (or write directly to *Guide Emer,* 50, rue Quai de L'Hôtel de Ville, 75004, Paris). The *Guide* lists dealers by region and by specialty, including dealers in antique tile, stonework, wrought iron, lace, and paneling, and no serious collector would make a buying trip in France without it. Three other useful publications are the magazines *ABC Décor, Trouvailles,* and *Estampille,* sold in bookstores and at many newsstands in France; in addition to interesting, in-depth features on French antiques and collectibles, they give the dates of antiques shows and fairs taking place throughout France.

IN PROVENCE

Les Antiquaires du Paradou
13520 Le Paradou,
Bouches-du-Rhône

Maison de la Tour
13990 Fontvielle,
Bouches-du-Rhône

Le Mas de Curebourg
84800 l'Isle-sur-la-Sorgue,
Vaucluse

Le Mas Saint-Roch
13125 Le Paradou,
Bouches-du-Rhône

M. Mouisson
Mas de la Monaque
13520 Maussane-
les-Alpilles,
Bouches-du-Rhône

IN THE LOIRE VALLEY

M. Metzger
49420 Pouance,
Maine-et-Loire

IN NORMANDY

Cherpitel
Château de l'Isle Manlère
50300 St. Quentin-sur-le-
Homme (near Avranches),
Manche

IN PARIS

Louvre des Antiquaires
Place du Palais Royal
75001 Paris

Marche Suisse
Michel Ottin, President
78, Avenue de Suffren
75015 Paris

*At the Marche
aux Puces
(Flea Market),
Saint Ouen*

Daniel Mayer
Cambo—Stand 18
Rue des Rosiers

M. Barbera
Marche Cambo—Stand 19
Rue des Rosiers

PROVENÇAL-STYLE FURNITURE REPRO-DUCTIONS

The two craftsmen listed below create fine artisanal reproductions of banquettes, chairs, and other typical pieces of Provençal furniture, each as carefully handworked as the originals.

Canteroux
Avenue d'Espagne
66000 Perpignan,
Pyrénées-Orientales

René Lacroix
4, boulevard Emile-Jamais
30300 Vallabrègues, *Gard*

BASKETWORK

The *vannerie,* or basketwork, specialists mentioned here weave baskets of all dimensions, from dainty baskets suitable for holding a boudoir potpourri to great vendage baskets designed to accommodate an afternoon's worth of harvested grapes. All offer a wide selection of market baskets.

**Albert Berton et
René Philippeau**
I'Île d'Elle
85770 Vix, *Vendée*

Christian Planton
Pondaurat
33190 La Réole, *Gironde*
Tel.: (56) 61.22.27

Comptoir Viticole
Petit place Carnot
21200 Beaune, *Côte d'Or*

Diot
36, place Madeleine
21200 Beaune, *Côte d'Or*

La Fabrique
25, avenue de la Libération
13210 Saint-Rémy,
Bouches-du-Rhône

Jean Crouzet
Vannerie
30300 Vallabrègues, *Gard*

**Société Coopérative
Agricole de Vannerie**
Villaines les Rochers
37190 Azay-le-Rideau,
Indre-et-Loire

BEADED CURTAINS

M. Darasse, working directly across the Rhône from Avignon, creates beaded curtains similar to the one pictured on page 82.

M. Darasse
Au Bout de Pont
30400 Villeneuve-lès-
Avignon, *Gard*

FAÏENCE

All kinds of pottery, from great terra-cotta urn planters to marbled-clay teapots to whimsically patterned plates and platters, are offered by the following faïence producers and stores.

Arts Ceram
La Fontaine
37380 Monnaie,
Indre-et-Loire
Tel.: (47) 56.10.78

Atelier de Ségriès
04360 Moustiers-
Sainte-Marie,
*Alpes-de-Haute-
Provence*
Tel: (92) 74.66.69

Céramique Terre à Feu
Place Montfort
84110 Vaison-la-Romaine,
Vaucluse

Ets Boisset
Pots d'Anduze
30140 Anduze, *Gard*

Faïences de Paris
Z. I. quartier de la Gare
83110 Sanary-sur-Mer, *Var*
Tel.: 74.50.19

Foulon
La Roche Vineuse
71960 Pierreclos,
Saône-et-Loire
Tel.: (85) 37.70.84

**Fourmaintraux et
Dutertre**
La Poterie
62240 Desvres,
Pas de Calais
Tel.: 91.65.55

Grindley
℅ Damay
5 bis, rue Martel
75010 Paris
Tel.: 824.71.73

Jean Benasso
B. P. 943
83050 Toulon, *Var*

**Jean Faucon,
Atelier Bernard**
12, avenue de la Libération
84400 Apt, *Vaucluse*

**Martel (Stenlle
des ets Geo)**
Chaussée Brundhaut
62240 Desvres,
Pas de Calais
Tel.: (21) 91.68.28

**Masse Artisans
Faïenciers**
B.P. 11
62240 Desvres,
Pas de Calais
Tel.: (21) 91.63.99

Pierre Vincent
C.D. 190 Molières-
Cavaillac
30120 Le Vigan, *Gard*
Tel.: (66) 91.14.01

**Poterie de
Haute-Provence**
Route de Nyons
26220 Dieulefit, *Drôme*
Tel.: (75) 46.42.10

Poterie Montgolfier
Avenue d'Angers
49430 Durtal,
Maine-et-Loire
Tel.: (16 37) 26.74.11

**Potterie Schmitter
Roger-Edmond**
18, rue de la Poste
67660 Betschdorf,
Rhin (Bas)
Tel.: (88) 54.42.44

P. Sourdive
26620 Cliousclat, *Drôme*

Schneider-Soeurs
76, avenue de
Maréchal-Juin
06400 Cannes,
Alpes-Maritimes

GLASSWARE

Provincial glassware with an artisanal look, for example, the chunky goblets of Biot with tiny bubbles in the subtly tinted glass, is available from the firms listed below. The last source included—Vincent Mit l'Ane—sells a variety of antique glassware.

La Rochère
Passavant-La Rochère
70210 Vauvillers,
Saône (Haute)
Tel.: (84) 68.08.12

S.A.T.
130, avenue Maréchal-Leclerc
33130 Bègles, *Gironde*
Tel.: (56) 85.19.93

Verrerie de Biot
Chemin des Combes
06410 Biot,
Alpes-Maritimes
Tel.: (93) 65.03.00

Verreries du Gier
Rue Joseph-Hermain
42800 Rive-de-Gier, *Loire*
Tel.: (77) 75.05.34

Verreries Mécaniques Champenoises
41, rue Pierre-Maître
51100 Reims, *Marne*
Tel.: (26) 87.96.00

Vincent Mit l'Ane
Route d'Apt
84800 l'Isle-sur-la-Sorgue,
Vaucluse
Tel.: (90) 38.07.37
Antique glassware

HERBS, CANDLES, SOAPS, DRIED FLOWERS

A heady assortment of dried herbs and flowers, as well as naturally scented products such as lavender soap, floral oils, and beeswax candles, can be purchased from the shops listed below.

Ateliers de la Garrigue
B.P. 7
34270 Lauret, *Hérault*
Tel.: (67) 55.24.12

Comptoir sud Pacifique
34, place du
Marche-Saint-Honoré
75001 Paris
Tel.: (1) 261.06.76

Distillerie de Lure
04100 Forcalquiers,
Alpes-de-Haute-Provence

Domaine de la Motte
30800 Saint-Gilles, *Gard*
Tel.: (66) 87.34.45

Epigone
1640, chemin de la Plaine
Zone Industrielle
06250 Mougins,
Alpes-Maritimes
Tel.: (93) 75.78.73

Le Jardin Retrouvé
3, cour Jasmin
75016 Paris
Tel.: (1) 527.70.31

Poterie des Herbiers
4, avenue E.-Herriot
91440 Bures-sur-Yvette,
Essone
Tel.: 446.96.17

M. Rampal
71, rue Félix-Piat
13300 Salon-de-Provence,
Bouches-du-Rhône

PEWTER

If you're in the market for pewter presentation plates, sconces, candlesticks, coffeepots, or other items in solid, provincial-looking pewter, these firms offer a wide variety of items in this popular, durable metal.

Étains à la Licorne Credor
14, rue Manin
75109 Paris
Tel.: 208.42.47

Les Étains de France
129, rue Saint-Leonard
49009 Angers,
Maine-et-Loire
Tel.: (41) 66.56.80

Étains de l'Echauguette
382, rue A.-Briant
62150 Houdain,
Pas-de-Calais
Tel.: (21) 62.57.16

Étains de la Fontaine
8, avenue J.-Mermoz
93120 La Courneuve,
Seine St. Denis
Tel.: 836.48.67

Étains de l'Ostrevent
28, rue A.-France
59490 Somain, *Nord*
Tel.: (27) 86.12.34

Étains de la Palmette
42, rue P.-Brossolette
93130 Noisy-le-Sec,
Seine St. Denis
Tel.: 846.45.71

Étains de Paris
13, rue Gambetta
95320 Saint-Leu-la-Forêt,
Val d'Oise
Tel.: 960.83.55

Étains du Manoir
CIAT Bureau 109
32, rue de Paradis
75010 Paris
Tel.: 246.62.61

Étains du Prince
17, boulevard Henri-IV
63600 Ambert,
Pay-de-Dôme
Tel.: (73) 82.08.69

Étains du Rouergue
12260 Villeneuve-d'Aveyron, *Aveyron*
Tel.: (65) 45.64.03

Étains J. Sitoleux
17, rue Guenot
75011 Paris
Tel.: 370.59.45

PROVINCIAL FABRICS

Traditional regional French fabrics from areas such as Provence and Alsace, and/or Paris-designed fabrics with a provincial look, created to complement any kind of country setting, are available from the following producers and stores.

Charles Deméry
1, rue Lobineau
75006 Paris

Charles Deméry
39, rue Proudhon
13150 Tarascon,
Bouches-du-Rhône

Deschemaker
22, rue du Mail
75002 Paris
Tel.: 233.35.80

Houles et Cie
18, rue St. Nicolas
75012 Paris

Lauer—Tapis de Cogolin
5, avenue de l'Opéra
75001 Paris
Tel.: 260.61.16

Manuel Canovas
7, rue Furstenberg
75006 Paris

Manufacture d'Impression sur Étoffes
19, route de Ste. Marie
aux Mines
68150 Ribeauville,
Rhin (Haut)
Tel.: (89) 73.74.74 (W)

Pierre Frey
47, rue des Petits-Champs
75001 Paris
Tel.: 297.44.00

Prelle
5, place des Victoires
75001 Paris
Tel.: 236.67.21

Romanex de Boussac
27, rue du Mail
75002 Paris
Tel.: 233.46.88

S. A. Burger et Cie.
39, rue des Petits-Champs
75001 Paris (W)

Les Tissus Casal
40, rue des Saints-Pères
75007 Paris
Tel.: 544.78.70 (W)

Tissus Fontan
38 et 40, rue Bonaparte
75006 Paris

SANTONS

The following *santonniers* create charming santons in a broad range of sizes, colors, and styles, from miniature hand-molded, hand-painted figures in terracotta to large, doll-size creations with hand-stitched Provençal costumes.

Elisabeth Ferriol
31, rue Voltaire
13200 Arles,
Bouches-du-Rhône
Tel.: (90) 96.69.81

Georges Cursat
Chemin de la Vieille Font
13990 Fontvieille,
Bouches-du-Rhône

Les Ateliers Marcel Carbonel
84-86, rue Grignan
13001 Marseille,
Bouches-du-Rhône
Tel.: (91) 54.26.58

P. Fouque
65 cours Gambetta
13100 Aix-en-Provence,
Bouches-du-Rhône

Santons Escoffier et Fils
43, boulevard Boisson
13004 Marseille,
Bouches-du-Rhône
Tel.: (16 91) 34.10.39

SCOURTINS
(HEMP OLIVE-OIL FILTERS)

Georges Fert weaves
sturdy, versatile hemp
olive-oil filters, popular
as place mats, doormats,
or wall decorations in
the south of France.

Georges Fert
Quartier de la Maladrerie
26110 Nyons, *Drôme*

TILES

The following firms pro-
duce glazed and
unglazed provincial tiles,
some patterned, some
plain. The brilliant, multicolored enameled tiles
of François Vernin are
featured on page 145.

Cazeaux
15, rue de Larreguy
64200 Biarritz-la Negresse,
Pyrenées-Atlantique

**François Vernin
Carreaux d'Apt**
Le Pont Julien,
84400 Bonnieux, *Vaucluse*

Lambert
Route de Chalon
71550 Chagny,
Saône-et-Loire

**Tuillerie Forge
Mayle-David**
Morizes
33190 La Réole, *Gironde*

IN ENGLAND
ANTIQUE FURNITURE

This is a selective listing:
for further information
consult the British Art &
Antiques Directory, pub-
lished by The Antique
Collector, National Maga-
zine House, 72 Broad-
wick Street, London W1V
2BP, tel: 439 7144 or The
British Antique Dealers'
Association, 20 Rutland
Gate, London SW7 1BD,
tel: 589 4128

Alexander & Berendt
1A Davies St.
London W1Y 1LL
Tel.: 499 4775

H. Blairman & Sons Ltd
119 Mount St.
London W1Y 5HB
Tel.: 493 0444

I. & J.L. Brown
636 King's Rd.
London SW6 2DU
Tel.: 736 4141

Buck & Payne
5 Camden Passage
London N1 8EH
Tel.: 226 4326

Tony Bunzl & Zal Davar
344 King's Rd.
London SW3 5UR
Tel.: 352 3697

**Mallett at Bourdon
House**
2 Davies St.
Berkeley Square
London W1Y 1LJ
Tel.: 629 2444

Partridge (Fine Arts) Ltd
144–146 New Bond St.
London W1Y OLY
Tel.: 629 0834

William Redford
9 Mount St.
London W1Y 5AD
Tel.: 629 1165

SOULEIADO FABRICS

The sole outlet in the
UK is:

Souleiado
171 Fulham Rd.
London SW3 6JW
Tel.: 589 6180

FABRICS AND WALL COVERINGS

These sources offer a
variety of fabrics and
wallcoverings, antique
and new, in provincial
styles. For more informa-
tion and outlets contact
the West End Furnishing
Fabrics Association, 25
Bedford Row, London
WC1R 4HN, tel: 242
6171.

Descamps
197 Sloane St.
London SW1X 9QX
Tel.: 235 6957

Designers Guild
277 King's Rd.
London SW3 5EN
Tel.: 370 5001

**International Linen
Promotion**
31 Great Queen St.
London WC2B 5AA
Tel.: 405 7791

Laura Ashley
183 Sloane St.
London SW1X 9QP
Tel.: 235 9728

Marvic Textiles
12–14 Mortimer St.
London W1N 7RD
Tel.: 580 7951

Mary Fox Linton
249 Fulham Rd.
London SW3 6HY
Tel.: 351 0273

Osborne & Little
304 King's Rd.
London SW3 5UH
Tel.: 352 1456

H.A. Percheron Ltd
97–99 Cleveland St.
London W1P 5PN
Tel.: 580 5156

Tissunique Ltd
10 Princes St.
Hanover Square
London W1R 7RD
Tel.: 491 3386

COOKWARE AND TABLEWARE

**The Antique Porcelain
Company Ltd**
149 New Bond St.
London W1Y OHY
Tel.: 629 1254

Divertimenti
68–72 Marylebone La.
London W1M 5FF
Tel.: 935 0689

Elizabeth David Ltd
46 Bourne St.
London SW1W 8JD
Tel.: 730 3123

The French Kitchen
42 Westbourne Grove
London W2 5RT
Tel.: 229 5530

TILES

Fired Earth
102 Portland Rd.
London W11 4LX
Tel.: 221 4825

Paris Ceramics
543 Battersea Park Rd.
London SW11 3BL
Tel.: 228 5785

Tile Mart
151 Great Portland St.
London W1N 5FB
Tel.: 580 3814

BASKETS

A number of contempo-
rary craftspeople make
good quality baskets. The
Crafts Council at 12
Waterloo Place, London
SW1Y 4AU (tel: 930
4811), will supply a list of
stocklists.

LARGE STORES

Quality shops that sell a
comprehensive range of
merchandise for interiors
and may offer an interior
design service (for information on free-lance in-
terior designers contact
the Interior Decorators
& Designers Association
(DDA) 45 Sheen Lane,
London SW14 8AB, tel:
876 4415/6).

Conran Shop
77–79 Fulham Rd.
London SW3 6RE
Tel.: 589 7401

Habitat
206–222 King's Rd.
London SW3 5XP
Tel.: 351 1211

Harrods
Knightsbridge
London SW1X 7XL
Tel.: 730 1234

Harvey Nichols
109–125 Knightsbridge
London SW1X 7RJ
Tel.: 235 5000

Heal's
196 Tottenham Court Rd.
London W1P 9LD
Tel.: 636 1666

Liberty & Co
210–220 Regent St.
London W1 6AH
Tel.: 734 1234

INDEX

© Charles Deméry